T0316651

# Cambridge Elements ≡

Elements in Organization Theory
edited by
Nelson Phillips
*Imperial College London*
Royston Greenwood
*University of Alberta*

# EMOTIONS IN ORGANIZATION THEORY

Charlene Zietsma
*Pennsylvania State University*

Madeline Toubiana
*University of Alberta*

Maxim Voronov
*York University, Canada*

Anna Roberts
*Pennsylvania State University*

CAMBRIDGE
UNIVERSITY PRESS

# CAMBRIDGE
## UNIVERSITY PRESS

University Printing House, Cambridge CB2 8BS, United Kingdom

One Liberty Plaza, 20th Floor, New York, NY 10006, USA

477 Williamstown Road, Port Melbourne, VIC 3207, Australia

314–321, 3rd Floor, Plot 3, Splendor Forum, Jasola District Centre, New Delhi – 110025, India

79 Anson Road, #06–04/06, Singapore 079906

Cambridge University Press is part of the University of Cambridge.

It furthers the University's mission by disseminating knowledge in the pursuit of education, learning, and research at the highest international levels of excellence.

www.cambridge.org
Information on this title: www.cambridge.org/9781108468237
DOI: 10.1017/9781108628051

© Charlene Zietsma, Madeline Toubiana, Maxim Voronov and Anna Roberts 2019

First published 2019

*A catalogue record for this publication is available from the British Library.*

ISBN 978-1-108-46823-7 Paperback
ISSN 2397-947X (online)
ISSN 2514-3859 (print)

Cambridge University Press has no responsibility for the persistence or accuracy of URLs for external or third-party internet websites referred to in this publication and does not guarantee that any content on such websites is, or will remain, accurate or appropriate.

# Emotions in Organization Theory

Elements in Organization Theory

DOI: 10.1017/9781108628051
First published online: March 2019

Charlene Zietsma
*Pennsylvania State University*

Madeline Toubiana
University of Alberta

Maxim Voronov
*York University, Canada*

Anna Roberts
*Pennsylvania State University*

**Author for correspondence:** Charlene Zietsma, czietsma@psu.edu

**Abstract:** Emotions are central to social life, and thus they should be central to organization theory. However, emotions have been treated implicitly rather than theorized directly in much of organization theory, and in some literatures, they have been ignored altogether. This Element focuses on emotions as intersubjective, collective and relational, and reviews structuralist, people-centered and strategic approaches to emotions in different research streams to provide one of the first broad examinations of emotions in organization theory. Charlene Zietsma, Madeline Toubiana, Maxim Voronov and Anna Roberts provide suggestions for future research within each literature and look across the literatures to identify theoretical and methodological considerations.

**Keywords:** emotions, organization theory, social emotions

Isbns: 9781108468237 (PB), 9781108628051 (OC)
Issns: 2397-947X (online), 2514-3859 (print)

# Contents

# 1 Introduction: Emotions in Organization Theory

## 1.1 Emotions in Organization Theory

Emotions are integral to social life, infusing, inspiring and shaping our actions and experiences (Goodwin & Pfaff, 2001; Voronov & Vince, 2012). They are the "glue binding people together," and they generate "commitments to large scale social and cultural structures" (Turner & Stets, 2005: 1). Emotions are deeply connected to social processes at societal, interorganizational, organizational and interpersonal levels. However, in much of organization theory, emotions, if considered at all, have been treated implicitly, or considered secondary to cognitive dynamics. This is problematic, because, as Jasper has suggested: "all the cultural models and concepts in use (e.g. frames, identities, narratives) are mis-specified if they do not include explicit emotional causal mechanisms" (Jasper, 2011: 286). In this Element, we set out to examine the state of research on emotions in organization theory. We do this with the dual objective of illuminating the extant work in this domain and highlighting opportunities for future research.

We argue that because emotions are central to organizational processes and social behavior, they should be seen as central to organization theory. Emotions have structural impacts: they are an important component of the connection between people and their networks (Granovetter, 1973; Mische, 2011; Uzzi, 1997) and social groups (Voronov & Yorks, 2015; Wright, Zammuto & Liesch, 2017). They structure and are structured by the norms, practices, beliefs, values and rules associated with their social groups (Keltner & Haidt, 1999), serving as a means by which people consciously or unconsciously self-regulate their behavior to meet societal norms (Creed et al., 2014).

Emotions also have strategic uses: they contribute to dynamic processes of organizational or institutional change, and they are heavily implicated in efforts to achieve stability, or to protect or promote values (Toubiana & Zietsma, 2017; Vaccaro & Palazzo, 2015; Wright et al., 2017). Emotions can be used strategically to incite or to suppress mobilization of activism (Poletta & Jasper, 2001; Moisander, Hirsto & Fahy, 2016) or to strengthen people's connection to groups (Collins, 2004) or to products and markets (Massa et al., 2017; Weber, Heinze & DeSoucey, 2008). Employers can require employees to express certain emotions at work as well (Hochschild, 1979; Rafaeli & Sutton, 1987), and individuals can use emotional displays to show their competence in a social domain (; Goffman, 1959; Voronov & Weber, 2016).

One can also consider the effects of emotions on people: emotions fuel efforts to resist or engage in organizational change (Huy, Corley & Kraatz, 2014; Vince, 2006) and institutional work (Voronov & Vince, 2012). They affect organizational learning (Gabriel & Griffiths, 2002) and other organizational outcomes such as risk-taking, teamwork and employee satisfaction (Barsade & O'Neill, 2014; O'Neill & Rothbard, 2017). They enable people with diverse perspectives to work together (Fan & Zietsma, 2017), and they drive groups with diverse perspectives apart (Toubiana & Zietsma, 2017).

Thus, it is apparent that emotions are fully intertwined with social life (Grodal, Nelson & Siino, 2015), having causal effects that can be frequently ignored when researchers consider only cognitive drivers of behavior. Organizational theories that ignore emotions are missing a tremendously rich source of influence on social dynamics. Enriching our theories with a better understanding of emotions and their influences represents an important challenge and opportunity for organization theory researchers.

Yet emotions have not been entirely ignored in organization theory. Some research streams have taken up emotions quite enthusiastically, while others have barely acknowledged them. Though much has been written about emotions in organizations in certain domains, there has not been a systematic review of emotions in organization theory more generally. There is a need for a comprehensive review that goes above and beyond analyzing emotions for one particular area of study and brings together our use and understanding of emotions across the literatures in organization theory. Seeking to fill this gap, this Element highlights the implicit and explicit roles of emotions in different organization theory research streams to provide one of the first broad examinations of emotions in this way.

### 1.1.1 A Sociological Approach to Emotions

This Element focuses on a sociological approach to emotions, which we believe is appropriate for studies in organization theory (for a history of sociological approaches to emotions, see Bericat, 2016; Stets & Turner, 2014; Turner & Stets, 2005;). A sociological approach to emotions is sensitive to the idea that emotions are experienced bodily by individuals (Bericat, 2016) in interaction with the social world (Collins, 2004, 2001), but understands them to be socially structured by conventions and culture (Gould, 2009), and experienced relationally (Emirbayer, 1997; Mische, 2011). Emotions are often collectively produced in interactions (Collins, 2004), socially contagious (Barsade, 2002) and easily amplified (Hallet, 2003). We experience and express emotions and interpret other's emotions based on the norms and cultural practices associated with our social contexts and interactions, with the understanding that emotions such as anger or love will be experienced and expressed differently in different contexts and between different people (Illouz, Gilon & Shachak, 2014). We experience fear, anger, hope, happiness or even sexual desire in alignment with our habitus (Bourdieu, 2000; Friedland, 2018), our social groups, our gender (see Figure 1), race, class etc. Even whether or not people engaging in sexual acts experience

**Figure 1** Hugs, Robot. "Emotions." Cartoon. *Robot Hugs*. July 21, 2015. www.robot-hugs.com/emotions/

Gender and emotions: Men and women are expected to display emotions differently based on culturally defined gender roles. These cultural norms can have negative effects on both men and women, as this article and comic strips suggest: www.upworthy.com/a-short-comic-strip-explains-how-our-double-standard-about-feelings-hurts-men-too?c=ufb5.

Women in particular are socialized against displaying anger, or displaying it in only very restrained ways: www.nytimes.com/2018/01/17/magazine/i-used-to-insist-i-didnt-get-angry-not-anymore.html?emc=edit_th_180121&nl=todayshea dlines&nlid=80012837, as actress Uma Thurman displays in this video: https://youtu.be/Rs4gK8DuuWY.

Beyond the regulation of one's own emotions, another article discusses President Donald Trump's "work wives." Author Jill Filipovic argues that: "Assumptions that women will monitor and manage men's emotions span industries and political persuasions. It's not that subtly sexist men refuse wholesale to hire women; it's that they often hire a small number of us, with the unspoken but swiftly understood expectation that we will be the uncompensated 'chief feelings officer.' Then they often lose respect for us because we play this very role." www.nytimes.com/2018/01/20/opinion/donald-trump-and-his-work-wives.html?emc=edit_th_180121&nl=to daysheadlines&nlid=80012837

orgasm is related to their religious and ideological beliefs and affiliation (Friedland et al., 2014). Thus, we focus on emotions as intersubjective, collective and relational – conditioned by one's place in the social world and one's relationship with others, especially the groups to which one belongs.

A sociological approach to emotions stands in contrast to approaches to emotion that dominate in psychology and organizational behavior. While definitional disputes continue (Gooty, Gavin & Ashkanasy, 2009), most researchers in more psychological traditions largely agree that emotions are intrapersonal "reaction[s] to a stimulus" with "a range of possible consequences" (Frijda, 1988; Elfenbein, 2007: 317). Such work emphasizes "feeling states and physiological changes" (Elfenbein, 2007: 315) elicited by stimuli, devoid of context and culture (Fineman, 2004; Haidt, 2012), though recognition within psychology and organizational behavior is growing that the emotional registration process is deeply contextualized (Ashforth & Kreiner, 2014; Brescoll & Uhlmann, 2008; Gooty et al., 2009). However, despite the importance of this work, Voronov (2014: 172) warns, emotions as conceptualized in a traditional psychological approach can present ontological problems for a sociology of emotions, since "both emotions and people – or individuals – are reified and extracted from their social context," and laboratory experiments are thought to be able to "reveal basic properties of emotions that would, theoretically, still hold regardless of the specific real world properties of these stimuli." Such psychological approaches are incompatible with sociological ontologies of emotions, which see them as relationally produced and culturally constituted. Accordingly, in this Element, we adopt a more sociological approach to emotions, while acknowledging that differing perspectives on emotions are prevalent in organizational behavior and in some of the work we cite.

### 1.1.2 The Emergence of Emotions in Organization Theory

As Gabriel and Griffiths write (2002: 2014): "Far from being emotional deserts, organizations are full of emotion and passion." From the beginning, emotions have been an implicit part of organization theory. Weber's value rationality incorporates "the actor's specific affects and feeling states" (Weber, 1978: 25), and his notion of charismatic authority relies on genuine emotional support. Heralding the beginning of the human relations movement, Mary Parker Follett focuses on the relationship between workers and managers and the "law of the situation," foreshadowing later work on organizational culture (Follett, 1927). Barnard (1938) built on these ideas to discuss the creation of a persuasive moral code for workers, inspiring "morale" to secure workers' "willing" cooperation. Gouldner (1954) shows how the informal organization, involving kinship-like connections and good sentiments between management and workers, was an important part of the functioning of a mine, and significant strife resulted when a replacement manager relied only on the formal organization. Selznick (1957: 17) argues that institutionalization occurs when structures, organizations and activities become "infused" with affect and "value beyond the technical requirements at hand." Despite these emotional underpinnings, few organization theories explicitly focused on emotions as central to their theorizing. Particularly as cognitive approaches in organization theory began to challenge hyperrational approaches (e.g., DiMaggio & Powell, 1983; March & Simon, 1958; Meyer & Rowan, 1977), emotions remained out of focus.

By the late 1970s, Hochschild's research on the sociology of emotions (1979, 1983), introducing the concepts of feeling rules, feeling display rules and emotional labor, sparked a flurry of organizational behavior research into the role that emotions play in organizational settings (see, e.g., Rafaeli and Sutton, 1987, 1989; Sutton & Rafaeli, 1988). Building on this foundation, a healthy literature has burgeoned around emotions and organizations at the individual level (see Elfenbein, 2007; Grandey, 2008; Gooty et al., 2009; Ashkanasy & Dorris, 2017, for literature reviews). Concepts such as emotional intelligence (e.g., Mayer & Salovey, 1997; Joseph & Newman, 2010; Dong, Seo & Bartol, 2014; see Fineman, 2004, and Matthews, Zeidner & Roberts, 2002, for critiques), emotional contagion (e.g., Kelly & Barsade, 2001; Barsade, 2002; Hareli & Rafaeli, 2008), group emotions (e.g., Menges & Kilduff, 2015) and the role of emotion in leadership (e.g., Bono et al., 2007; Toegel, Kilduff & Anand, 2013) have emerged. However, as we are focused on organization theory and a more sociological view of emotions, we consider these various strands of organizational behavior literature out of scope and do not delve into them in this Element.

Instead, we are concerned with organizations, organizing and more macro levels of analysis. While the lines are not always easily drawn, we attempt to remain firmly rooted in theories traditionally considered as comprising the canon of organization theory.

## 1.1.3 Organization of This Element

Organization theory includes a range of literatures at various levels of analysis, and demarcations between organization theory and related disciplines such as organizational behavior, sociology and strategy are not always clear. Our approach to identifying key organization theory topics or theoretical perspectives involves examining the topics submission list for the 2016 and 2017

Academy of Management Conference in the Organization and Management Theory (OMT) Division, and surveying recent organization theory doctoral course syllabi. We then review each of these theoretical perspectives to identify literature related to emotions within each topic. In this Element, we classify each theoretical perspective according to the extent of its consideration of emotions. Literatures where there is *substantial* work on emotions include institutional theory, social movement theory, identity theory, organizational culture, power and control and organizational learning, routines and change. Literatures featuring more *limited* work on emotions include sensemaking, practice theory, networks and entrepreneurship. Literatures in which emotions are nearly *absent* from theorizing include the topics of organizational economics (agency theory and transaction cost economics), economic sociology and embeddedness, organizational ecology, categories and resource dependence theory.

Within each reviewed theoretical area, we adopt a common approach. In a rich and comprehensive review of the emotional work in institutional theory, Lok et al. (2017) develop a categorization scheme regarding the role of emotions in the studies they reviewed. They identify three different perspectives in studying emotions: *structuralist, people-centered* and *strategic*, and further segment them into change and reproduction. While the change and reproduction aspects are particularly germane to institutional theory and not as broadly applicable, we feel the *structuralist, people-centered* and *strategic* perspectives they articulate have broader application – they transcend institutional theory to apply to all of organization theory. We thus borrow and adapt this categorization scheme to review the literature in each theoretical stream and generate future research directions.

*Structuralist perspectives* are those that consider how emotions are constituted in (and constitutive of) social structures – that is, how they are "integral to their purposive, animating force" (Lok et al., 2017: 33). For example, emotions such as faith and hope are a significant component of religious institutions (Gutierrez et al., 2010), while caring is embedded in the professional norms of medical professionals (Wright et al., 2017), and organizations can have particular emotional cultures, with significant organizational effects (Barsade & O'Neill, 2014; O'Neill & Rothbard, 2015). *People-centered perspectives* focus on people's emotional responses and reactions to organizations and organizing dynamics (Petriglieri, Ashford & Wrzesniewski, in press). For example, such approaches focus on the anxiety or resistance employees experience when faced with an organizational change program (Smollan & Sayers, 2009), the positive emotions that come from identification with an organization (Dukerich, Golden &

Shortell, 2002), or the collective outrage groups experience when their expectations are violated (Toubiana & Zietsma, 2017). Finally, *strategic perspectives* focus on the use of emotions as "resources or tools" (Lok et al., 2017: 38) to affect others, for example, in using affective work to persuade them (Tracey, 2016), or in using smiling and other aspects of emotional labor to deliver customer service (Hochschild, 1979).

Within each review of a theory, we briefly outline the theory, review recent literature that deals with emotions within that theoretical perspective, then assess it based on its focus on structuralist, people-centered and strategic perspectives. Importantly, we find that many of the research streams take two of these perspectives, such as strategic use of emotions to effect people-centered responses, or people-centered responses arising from emotions constituted in structures, but not the third. We then reflect on what was absent in the literature, both based on our categorization scheme and, more broadly, to identify directions for future research.

### 1.1.4 Looking across the Theoretical Perspectives

In the final Section of this Element, we look across the theoretical perspectives to consider the role of emotions in organization theory as a whole. We connect emotions in theorizing with the ontological assumptions of the various theories to discuss theoretically appropriate directions for future research on emotions within and across literatures. We also discuss methodological challenges to studying emotions using a sociological view and consider some of the more innovative approaches we noted in our literature review to capture emotions empirically.

Our final arguments reiterate the importance of emotion for social theorizing and the importance of such theorizing to help us understand the world around us. Emotions have substantial influence in society: politically, organizationally, economically – indeed in every facet of life. The late emergence of emotion work in much organizational theorizing has impoverished our view of the world, we argue, and thus increased attention to emotions is critical to building a relevant and rigorous discipline.

## 2 Theories Featuring Substantial Work on Emotions: Institutional Theory, Social Movement Theory, Identity, Organizational Learning and Change, and Organizational Culture, Power and Control

### 2.1 Institutional Theory

Until very recently, emotions were absent in most neo-institutionalist studies. While multiple editions of Scott's (2014) classic book paved the way for an explicit theorizing about the role of emotions in institutions by suggesting that emotions may operate as a fourth pillar (Scott, 2001) or across the standard institutional regulative, normative and cognitive "pillars" (Scott, 2014), it was the increased interest in the micro-foundations of institutions that truly saw institutional theory shed its long-standing cognitive focus (for a review, see Lok et al., 2017, and Zietsma & Toubiana, 2018). Specifically, the institutional work and inhabited institutions perspectives triggered the recent flurry of research at the intersection of emotions and institutions. In the following sections, we discuss the use of emotions in institutional theory from strategic, people-centered and structuralist perspectives.

### 2.1.1 Strategic Use of Emotions by Actors to Maintain or Alter Institutions

Given the increased interest among institutional scholars in how people (or individuals) impact institutions, scholars have most frequently approached emotions from a strategic perspective. This work has shown how emotions can spark people to either maintain or try to transform institutional arrangements by constructing personally meaningful narratives (Creed, DeJordy & Lok, 2010; Gutierrez et al., 2010), and by using highly emotive, dramatic language to challenge established practices in field-configuring events (Schüssler, Rüling & Wittneben, 2014; Zietsma & Lawrence, 2010).

Further, recognizing the importance of emotive, value-based identity claims in legitimating accounts, Suddaby and Greenwood (2005: 56) explicitly argue that "[m]ost value-based rhetoric openly appeals, directly or indirectly, to emotion." However, their study does not explicitly factor in the strategic use of emotions by actors beyond the employment of value-based rhetoric. Other discursive studies have similarly highlighted the role of emotions (Brown, Ainsworth & Grant, 2012; Harmon, Green & Goodnight, 2015). In their study of an intermediary organization in rural Bangladesh, BRAC, Mair, Martí and Ventresca (2012: 839) describe how workers engaged in strategic action that involved making an emotional connection to produce institutional change:

> When POs visit households, they are usually offered . . . chairs or stools to sit. However, as a matter of strategy, POs instead of sitting on [a] stool/chair, sit on the ground. This makes the people embarrassed, but happy! They are embarrassed because they are not used to seeing an educated outsider sitting on the ground with them. But they are happy because the PO sits with them in an informal way as a nearer one which creates a fellow feeling among them and the gap becomes narrower.

While these studies did not incorporate emotions into their core theorizing, more recent discursive studies have done so. Conceptualizing emotions as discursive constructs, Moisander et al. (2016: 19) investigated "rhetorical strategies of emotion work – eclipsing, diverting and evoking emotions – through which institutional actors may seek to wield power in their attempts to manage resistance and to create support for their institutional projects." These discourses are only influential to the extent to which they resonate with audiences emotionally (Giorgi, 2017; Grodal & Granqvist, 2014; Haack, Pfarrer & Scherer, 2014). Similarly, Tracey's (2016) study of institutional "conversion" illustrates how the strategic use of emotions in rituals connects and commits people to particular institutional projects. Emotions can be not only expressed strategically in institutional work, but also deliberately suppressed. Jarvis, Goodrick and Hudson (forthcoming) show how animal rights activists elicited emotions among audiences by the use of visuals and videos, but suppressed their own emotions in order to shield themselves from being thought of as "irrational" and overly emotional. Emotions also have implications for embeddedness. Ruebottom and Auster (2018) demonstrate the importance of emotionally resonant rituals for disembedding actors from their institutional milieu in order to enable them to become change makers. Fan and Zietsma (2017) show the role of emotions in enabling dual embeddedness: the diverse actors they studied generated social and moral emotions and emotional energy while working together, enabling them to embed themselves in a new shared governance logic while remaining attached to their home logic.

Of course, one of the key roles of emotions in institutional processes is to animate and motivate the various forms of institutional work (Friedland, 2013; Voronov & Vince, 2012). Wright et al. (2017), for example, find that emergency department physicians, fueled by moral emotions, maintained their professional values by undertaking institutional work to advocate for patients. Other studies point to the role of emotions in institutional change. Public expression of emotion helped actors wrestle with a plethora of moral and legal issues in Lawrence's (in press) study of North America's first safe drug injection site. The pride felt by the first women students at the US Naval Academy enabled them to challenge and disrupt the institutionalized role prescriptions that applied to them, despite other's shaming and policing (DeJordy & Barrett, 2014). Martin de Holan, Willi and Fernández (in press) identify emotional resources as key to engaging in the work required to escape poverty. Massa et al. (2017) find that emotional investment, fueled by reverence, elation and awe, motivated institutional evangelism, which prompted practice dissemination. Farney, Kibler and Down (forthcoming) describe how collective emotions enabled institutional creation work in iterative cycles, serving both a justifying and a motivating function, in post-disaster recovery work in Haiti. Thus, emotions are strategically employed and deployed in institutional projects as resources to help actors shape institutions.

### 2.1.2 People-Centered Perspective: When Institutional Processes Trigger Emotional Responses

Institutional research has acknowledged implicitly for some time that emotions can be triggered in reaction to perceived threats to the values embedded in institutions (i.e., Lok & de Rond, 2013; Wright et al., 2017; Zilber, 2002). For instance, organizational actions that adhere to one logic may provoke negative emotional reactions from audiences that adhere to another logic (Lok, 2010; Marquis & Lounsbury, 2007). However, some researchers have begun to consider emotions from a people-centered perspective more explicitly, including Weber et al. (2008) in their study of the emergence of a market for grass-fed meat. The study focuses on how motivating frames, based on values, connected with emotional commitment. In the study, they state that: "Pioneering grass-fed producers chose and persisted with grass-based agriculture because they obtained emotional energy from connecting their work to a sense of self and moral values represented in the movement's codes" (Weber et al., 2008: 543). Hallett's (2010) study of institutional change in an elementary school, whereby the ideal of accountability was integrated into material classroom practices, offers a rich account of people's reactions to institutional disruption. In another example of the people-centered role of emotions, Voronov and Yorks (2015) argue that a key premise in institutional research, that institutional change is conditioned upon the presence of institutional contradictions (Seo & Creed, 2002), assumes that the contradictions are recognized by people. Yet such recognition is a highly emotive process and far from automatic (Haack & Sieweke, 2018). Exploring these issues empirically, Giorgi and Palmisano's (2017) study of mystic Catholics brings attention to the intensity of emotions in order to understand how persons' behaviors correspond to institutions. In their study, participants experienced intense emotions of joy, love and awe in their everyday institutional life, and these emotions prompted participants to set aside any tacitly rational calculations and cost-benefit analyses. In their study of a high-performing military medical team in Afghanistan, de Rond and Lok (2016) highlight how the breakdown of institutional arrangements can cause psychological trauma (see Video 1). Alternatively, people who experience events that threaten their continued emotional investment in an institutional order may shift the anchor of that emotional investment (Wijaya & Heugens,

2018) or engage in efforts to shame or shun those threatening these investments (Toubiana & Zietsma, 2017).

In many ways, the people-centric perspective on emotions has highlighted the ways in which emotions can enable or disable agency within institutions, which is why this perspective often overlaps with the strategic. For example, Jakob-Sadeh and Zilber (forthcoming) describe how a Jewish-Palestinian organization sought to control emotions in order to stabilize the internal constellation of logics under institutional complexity. However, emotions erupted at various times, disrupting logic constellations. Notably, members of the organization from an underprivileged group were limited in their ability to emotionally "erupt," suggesting power differences in the acceptability of emotional expression within a given context.

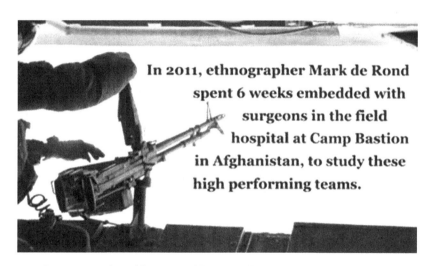

In 2011, ethnographer Mark de Rond spent 6 weeks embedded with surgeons in the field hospital at Camp Bastion in Afghanistan, to study these high performing teams.

**Video 1** Watch a video of a military medical team on a tour of duty in Afghanistan based on the research of Mark de Rond and Jako Lok's (2016) paper *Some Things Can Never Be Unseen*. Video Credit: Fred Lewsey, Cambridge University, www.youtube.com/watch?v=386JJ8Zj_CY.
Rights held by Mark de Rond. Used with permission.

### 2.1.3 Structuralist Perspective: Emotions Constituted in Institutions

While implicitly emotions have often been depicted in empirical studies as being constituted in institutions (see Lok et al., 2017, for an elaboration and examples), few studies have explicitly theorized the role of emotions from a structuralist perspective (Zietsma & Toubiana, 2018). This has begun to change, and several recent studies have started to advance this view of emotions in institutions. Voronov and Weber (2016, 2017) argue that emotions make institutional arrangements subjectively real to people. These arrangements are associated with specific emotions and they make other emotions unacceptable or illegitimate. Friedland (2018) advances a similar idea by suggesting intrinsic links between institutional logics and certain emotions. This has been and promises to be an important line of empirical inquiry. While a close reading of Thornton and Ocasio's (1999) influential study of changes in the publishing industry hints at the association of different logics with different emotions, Toubiana and Zietsma's (2017, see videos 2 and 3, also available at www .youtube.com/watch?v=F183G1zhB4g&t= and www.youtube.com/watch? v=2jPBzhkH_iU&t=) study shows that institutional logics are associated with specific emotional "registers" that regulate the use and expression of particular emotions.

**Video 2**  The Message Is on the Wall? Interview with Madeline Toubiana and Charlene Zietsma (www.youtube.com/watch?v=F183G1zhB4g&t).

Wright and colleagues (2017) illustrate how professions similarly can be infused with certain emotions. Gill and Burrow support this finding (2018) and show how fear is an inherent component of the institution of haute cuisine. Conversely, Delmestri and Goodrick (2017) argue that taken-for-grantedness, an important element of institutions, is conditional upon constant suppression of inappropriate or possibly institutionally disruptive emotions. Failure to experience and/or exhibit institutionally appropriate emotions can be destabilizing to

**Video 3** Emotions, Social Media and the Dynamics of Institutional Complexity Animation (www.youtube.com/watch?v=2jPBzhkH_iU&t).

Rights held by Madeline Toubiana and Charlene Zietsma. Used with permission.

the institutional arrangements (Creed et al., 2014; Jarvis, 2017), and reduce an actor's perceived competence within them (Voronov & Weber, 2017).

### 2.1.4 Directions for Future Research

Institutional theory already has begun to integrate the explicit study of emotions and stands to benefit from further such integration. In some senses, recent attention to emotions is simply a logical outcome of the increased interest in micro-foundations of institutions. These micro-foundation approaches, ranging from the inhabited perspective (Hallett & Ventresca, 2006), institutional work (Lawrence, Leca & Zilber, 2013), practice-based institutionalism (Smets, Aristidou & Whittington, 2017), to the micro-foundations of institutional logics (Thornton, Ocasio & Lounsbury, 2012), all bring people more strongly into analytic focus, and make ignoring emotions difficult. Emotions connect people to institutions and their institutional communities, and energize their agency (Zietsma & Toubiana, forthcoming).

Future research at the intersection of emotions and institutions could explore some of the following topics. First, incorporating emotions into institutional theory holds the promise to change our essential understanding of an institutional actor operating in institutions (Creed et al., 2014; Voronov & Weber, 2016). Future scholars may consider using emotions to contribute to institutional theory's notion of the actor and the conception of actors as embodied, bringing their whole selves – heart, mind and body – to the experience and enactment of institutions (Hallett & Ventresca, 2006). Michel (2011) posits that emotions connect the human body to institutions, a concept that enables researchers to explore further the social consequences of institutionalization of particular bodily constructions and experiences, such as race and gender. With this research focus, institutional theory would become increasingly capable of tackling important societal issues (Hudson, Okhuysen & Creed, 2015). Thus, the study of emotions and institutions reconceptualizes the actor not as boundedly rational, but as a more complete human being, inevitably driven (at least in part) by passions and desire (Vince, in press), connected to institutions (Friedland, 2018).

Second, attention to emotions helps to animate the resurgent interest in values among institutional scholars (Gehman, Trevino & Garud, 2013; Kraatz & Block, 2008). Values are institutionally conditioned and are made meaningful through emotions (Wright et al., 2017). In fact, some scholars suggest that the foundation of institutions is not cognition but ethos, or the moral-emotive character that defines a given institutional order (Voronov & Weber, 2016, 2017). Much research is needed, however, to establish the relationship between ethos and the traditional institutional constructs, such as logics (Toubiana, Greenwood & Zietsma, 2017). For instance, it is acknowledged that multiple institutional logics may at times coexist harmoniously and at other times be in tension. An intriguing possibility is that ethos could explain the extent to which logics coexist peacefully or are in conflict. For example, a capitalist ethos might establish a hierarchy and an orderly coexistence of logics by elevating the market logic to a privileged status in society vis-à-vis the family logic, whereby the latter might be supporting the former (Hochschild & Machung, 2012).

Third, institutional theory might help to advance the study of emotions in organizational research. At present, organizational scholarship on emotions is predominantly psychological in flavor. While the tendency to privilege the biological individual as the basic unit of analysis is valuable for understanding intrapersonal emotional experiences and discrete emotions, a sociological approach to emotions emphasizes that bodily experiences are not objective or essential, but are strongly mediated by culture (Gould, 2009), not only in interpretation but also in the bodily experiences that are possible or likely (Illouz et al., 2014). As Friedland (2018) noted, even whether one experiences an orgasm during sex depends on one's cultural conditioning. Failure to consider the social conditioning of intrapersonal experiences, and failure to consider more transpersonal and intersubjective emotional dynamics, limits social theory. The role of emotions as the social glue (Zietsma & Toubiana, forthcoming) that helps to organize and coordinate people within organizations and within society at large requires a more relational conceptualization of emotions (Emirbayer & Goldberg, 2005). Insights from institutional theory about emotions could be valuable. For instance, Wright et al. (2017) show how moral emotions might originate in professional norms, while Toubiana and Zietsma (2017) show that there is a particular emotional register associated with different institutional logics, which sets up the potential of intergroup/logic conflicts. Studies of interactions across different social groups have identified the importance of emotions such as excitement (Cartel, Boxenbaum & Aggeri, 2018), trust and liking (Fan & Zietsma, 2017), along with solidarity and emotional energy (Ruebottom & Auster, 2018), as increasing the potential for productive and integrative solutions to social problems (van Wijk et al., forthcoming), but significantly more work is required to define the emotions associated with embedding and disembedding, and how they might be strategically affected.

## 2.2 Social Movement Theory

Coordinating collective action is a central concern of social movements. Yet, while research on social movements is vast, a relatively small group of scholars has been pushing for increased attention to emotions, arguing that a failure to take emotions seriously in the study of social movements causes scholars to "fail to 'get the connections right'" (Emirbayer & Goldberg, 2005: 478) and to fail to grasp the "nuts and bolts" (Goodwin & Pfaff, 2001: 301) of the social movements processes. Accordingly, collective and relational manifestations of emotions are becoming central to research on social movements (Emirbayer & Goldberg, 2005). Goodwin, Jasper and Polletta's (2001) book, *Passionate Politics*, is a particularly important contribution to this domain, as it makes a compelling and influential case for the importance of incorporating emotions into the study of social movements and contentious politics.

The push to make emotions a central concern among social movement scholars is bearing fruit, and social movement scholars have offered some of the most sophisticated treatments of social and relational emotions. Thus, while more psychologically oriented researchers tend to view emotions as short-term and fleeting visceral reactions, social movement scholars have cast such "reflex emotions" (Jasper, 2011: 287) (including anger, fear, joy etc.) as only a part of the story. These, they argue, coexist with – and often depend on – other longer-term and more lasting emotional states, such as affective loyalties within a community and moral emotions (positive or negative feelings based on conformity or violations of shared moral codes) (Jasper, 2011). In what follows, we review the roles of emotions as conduits of collective action and mobilization, the role of emotions in facilitating social stability or change and their contributions to the formation of a collective identity.

### 2.2.1 Emotions and Mobilization

The most widely acknowledged role of emotions with respect to social movements is facilitation of mobilization, taking a primarily strategic view. Over the past three decades, social movement scholars have increasingly turned attention to the mechanisms that motivate people to rise up and take part in social movements. For instance, highly emotional speeches, whether reviled by opponents as terrifying or embraced by supporters as inspiring, helped mobilize supporters of prohibition, dropping liquor consumption dramatically and, thus, inadvertently shaping the legitimacy of soft drinks (Hiatt, Sine & Tolbert, 2009). Framing (Benford & Snow, 2000; Snow et al., 1986), whereby interpretative schemes of people are aligned – especially with respect to developing a common understanding of grievances and those responsible for them – is the dominant mechanism that has been identified. Framing facilitates the collective action needed to transform social arrangements that are deemed suboptimal and unfair. Framing, in fact, has become a very popular concept not only in social movements research but also in organization theory and management research more generally, used in research on institutions (Lounsbury, Ventresca & Hirsch, 2003; Rao, Monin & Durand, 2003), social judgments and legitimacy (Rhee & Fiss, 2014; Rindova, Pollock & Hayward, 2006), strategy process and practice (Kaplan, 2008) and other areas. Yet framing is not a purely cognitive process. Frames have to resonate with audiences, both cognitively and emotionally (Benford, 1997; Giorgi, 2017). For instance, Sine and Lee (2009: 136) find that the environmental movement directly and indirectly affected the emergence of the US wind energy sector and theorized that such effects were the result of the "construction and promulgation of these frames" through "affective processes of persuasion and socialization that seek to create shared values around which to build consensus." Recognizing the role of emotions as resources, social movement scholars are increasingly starting to study emotional bases of frame resonance, such as the types of emotional experiences invoked by frames that make the frames more or less conducive to mobilization (Bröer & Duyvendak, 2009; Schrock, Holden & Reid, 2004; Bergstrand, 2014).

Another common construct used to explain social mobilization is moral shock (Jasper & Poulsen, 1995), which activists use to convert apathetic bystanders into either participants or supporters of a social movement. Yet moral shock appears to be a double-edged sword, as some researchers have pointed out that it is likely to alienate rather than enroll some audience members (e.g., Scheff, 2007).

## 2.2.2 Emotions, Disruption and Stability

Attending to the people-centered dimension of emotions, social movement scholars have been keenly aware of the link between emotions and social disruption, whereby emotional reactions to phenomena prompt people to rise up: "Emotions do not simply lurk beneath the surface of, or arise in response to, 'real' processes of social change – they drive them, impede them, shape them, and furthermore, in some situations, they constitute the substance of social power" (Moon, 2013: 291). Though emotions are not explicitly theorized, social movement scholars studying contentious markets and the impact of social movements on controversial practices such as same-sex domestic partner benefits (Briscoe & Safford, 2008) implicitly rely upon differing emotional reactions by stakeholders as inherently disruptive in order to classify both the markets and the practices as contentious (King & Pearce, 2010). Conversely, there is increased acknowledgment that social stability is also grounded in emotional processes (Calhoun, 2001). Social movement scholars have acknowledged that people become attached to a status quo, and will actively defend it and suppress alternatives, because they are emotionally invested in current social arrangements (Moon, 2013).

Emotions might also keep social arrangements stable by keeping people paralyzed and unable to act as change agents. Gould (2009), for instance, notes the role of shame in keeping gay men from mobilizing to assert their rights in the face of the AIDS epidemic. Alternatively, emotions that might lead to the questioning of the status quo might be repressed (Delmestri & Goodrick, 2017). Emotions then can constrain people and hinder their capacity to either recognize or seize opportunities for action (Summers-Effler, 2002). Furthermore, commitment to a status quo is based not on a lack of emotions, but rather on emotional investment in the status quo (Calhoun, 2001). Social transformation then requires emotional energy and emotional liberation (Fan & Zietsma, 2017; Young, 2001; Benski & Langman, 2013).

## 2.2.3 Emotions and Collective Identity

Social movements often have to persist for a long time and against considerable adversity to accomplish their objectives – with no certainty of victory. As such, retaining members, and maintaining a collective identity within a movement is an important concern that has received considerable research attention (Polletta & Jasper, 2001). In the context of social movements, these collective identity processes are recognized as being profoundly emotion-laden. Social movement entrepreneurs build collective identities to resonate with and attract activists (Staggenborg, 2013; Rao, Morrill & Zald, 2000). As a result, social movement participants become and remain emotionally invested in the movement's goals (Calhoun, 2001) and remain committed to one another (Goodwin, 1997). Participating in social movements often involves partaking in interaction rituals that generate emotional energy and comradery among activists (Collins, 2001; Fan & Zietsma, 2017; Weber et al., 2008), which enables perseverance. This work emphasizes a people-centered approach to emotions, yet it is strongly linked to strategic and structural approaches.

An important recent extension on the theme is the recognition that social movements may not always act collectively by protesting or engaging in collective rituals. Rather, "others" might be virtually there – either in a remote technology-mediated locale (Massa, 2017) or as inspiration for the action of particular persons (Toubiana & Zietsma, 2017). For example, "lone wolf" terrorists, such as Anders Behring Breivik, who killed seventy-seven people in Norway, might appear to be acting as isolated "individuals" (www .telegraph.co.uk/news/2016/07/22/anders-breivik-inside-the-warped-mind-of-a-mass-killer/). Yet they are still embedded in a broader social movement that provides them with cultural toolkits both for understanding the world around them and for motivating their action (Berntzen & Sandberg, 2014). All this implies a recognition of the structural dimension of emotions, whereby social movements develop shared emotion cultures (Taylor & Rupp, 2002; Reger, 2004).

### *2.2.4 Directions for Future Research*

In summary, we see that while social movement research has yet to fully integrate emotions into the core of the research agenda, extant work has been broad-ranging – tackling strategic, people-centered and structuralist facets of emotions. While the themes discussed earlier feature emotions as underlying – and sometimes hidden – enablers of collective action, an exciting frontier would feature emotions as "ends" of collective action. Continuing with the exploration of the structuralist dimension of emotions, an important yet infrequently recognized insight is that social movements do not aim merely to transform material conditions. Rather, people may be motivated to engage in collective action by expressive needs. For example, both Christian conservative (Stein, 2001) and gay rights (Bernstein, 1997) activists may be motivated – at least in part – by the desire to stop feeling ashamed and to start feeling proud of who they are. Contestation then might aim to transform not only laws or other more tangible arrangements, but, instead, the feeling rules that do not permit experiencing positive emotions, such as pride, or experiencing pain that is deemed "illegitimate" (Kenney & Craig, 2012).

Groups may seek to transform not only the feeling rules that shape their own emotional experiences but also the emotional experiences of other groups, such as higher-status groups. For example, arguably the most meaningful way of ending discrimination against a certain group is not by outlawing discriminatory practices but by transforming how groups feel about each other, thereby replacing negative feelings with more positive or neutral ones.

If social movements are about social transformation, then attending to the role of social movements and collective action in transforming how societies feel about things is a natural direction to explore. A recent means of mobilization and transformation for social movements has been online organizing and influencing, sometimes aided by big data and artificial intelligence, as recent reports about Cambridge Analytica and its right-wing sponsors have made clear (https://arstechnica.com/tech-policy/2018/04/how-cambridge-analyticas-facebook-targeting-model-really-worked/), and future research is sorely needed in this area.

## 2.3 Identity

Identity has been a topic of importance in both the organization theory and organizational behavior literatures. Reviewing the extensive body of work within this literature is clearly beyond the scope of this Element. However, while emotions were, until recently, rarely central to empirical analysis (Conroy & O'Leary-Kelly, 2014; Pratt, 1998; Stets & Trettevik, 2014), a close look at the underpinnings of identity research reveals how tightly connected emotions are to identity dynamics. Thus, based on our review of the literature, we can identify three central elements of identity theorizing where emotions play a significant, if not always explicit, role: processes of identification, transition and social validation.

### 2.3.1 Identification Requires and Triggers Emotions

Identification is the process by which a given identity becomes self-defining (Ashforth, 2001; Ashforth et al., 2008; Vough, 2012). For example, organization identification "occurs when members perceive their own identity to overlap with their organization's identity, leading them to define themselves in terms of the organization and place a high value on organizational membership" (Besharov, 2014: 1485). Identification has been linked with a variety of outcomes such as commitment, helping behaviors and creativity, and is seen as crucial in linking the self to distinct social roles, groups and organizations (Ashforth et al., 2008; Besharov, 2014; Foreman & Whetten, 2002; Vough, 2012).

Attachment to being a member in a given identity group is expected to have "emotional significance" (Tajfel, 1978; Tajfel, 1982: 63; see Figure 2). Thus, emotion is central to identification, be it with a role, social group, organization or even a larger community. As Ashforth has outlined, "one can think or feel one's way into identification ... cognition and affect reciprocally reinforce identification" (2001: 329). This means that identification can be as much about how one feels about a social entity as it is about how much one thinks about it (Curchod, Patriotta & Neysen, 2014; Morales & Lambert, 2013; Sluss, van Dick & Thompson, 2011). There is call for further examination of the role of emotions in this regard, since, as Harquil and Wilcox King (2010: 1633) explain at the organizational level: "The body and emotions, as well as the mind, help to shape the motivation, strength, types, and quality of an individual's identity-based connection with an organization ... most models of organizational identification have no way to account for [this]."

Conversely, identification can trigger and generate emotions. The positive emotions derived or generated from identification can lead to positive engagement and citizenship behaviors, whether within an organization (Dukerich et al., 2002), or within a broader community (Howard-Grenville, Metzger & Meyer, 2013). Furthermore, identification can trigger negative emotions if the site of one's identification is threatened (Elsbach & Kramer, 1996; Gendron & Spira, 2010). For example, members of the Port Authority who were identified with the organization were angry and embarrassed when the Port Authority was depicted negatively in the news (Dutton & Dukerich, 1991). These types of negative emotions can lead those who identify with an organization to work to remedy the issues at hand so they can maintain at least partial identification with organizations or roles they hold as important (Creed et al., 2010; Gutierrez, Howard-Grenville & Scully, 2010; Leung, Zietsma & Peredo, 2014).

While emotions are thus often related to identification with organizations, professions or other clear targets, not having these traditional targets can also lead individuals to feel anxiety as they "lack a holding environment" or object for identification – something more prevalent with the emergence of the gig economy (Petriglieri, Ashford & Wrzesniewski, forthcoming; Roberts & Zietsma, 2018).

**Figure 2** At a football game with record attendance at Penn State University on October 21, 2017, nearly all of the more than 110,000 excited fans wore white to show support for (and strong identification with) their team in its game against rival University of Michigan.

Photo credit: Stephen Parkhill. Used with permission.

### 2.3.2 Emotions Related to Identity Transitions

Emotions feature most centrally in the discussions of identity transitions – that is situations where there is identity change, loss and/or adaptation. When preferred identities are threatened, actors have been observed to react with negative emotions (Corley & Gioia, 2004; Petriglieri, 2011, 2015), as threats to identity trigger "psychic pain, discomfort, anxiety, conflicts, and overall loss of self-esteem" (Gioia et al., 2013: 133), feelings that can lead to a sense of change overload (Corley & Gioia, 2004). This is similar, in many ways, to the threat response adopted by actors invested in institutions: "threatening highly meaningful identities engender[s] stronger negative emotions whereas events reinforcing such identities engender stronger positive emotions" (Cascón-Pereira & Hallier, 2012: 132). This focus on emotions as reactions is again a people-centric conceptualization of emotions.

Identity transitions often require efforts to let go of a past identity and to forge connections with a new identity (Ashforth, 2001; Conroy & O'Leary-Kelly, 2014;

Fiol, 2002; Hatch, Schultz & Skov, 2015; Obodaru, 2012, 2017; Toubiana, 2014). This involves "emotionally disentangl[ing]" oneself from the old identity (Ebaugh, 1988) – a process that is expected to be difficult and to require emotional regulation (Conroy & O'Leary-Kelly, 2014; Toubiana, 2014) as can the process of feeling connected to the new identity (Ibarra, 1999). Recovering and coping with the loss of a desired identity is an emotional process, as much as it is a cognitive one, and if actors are unable to manage these emotions, they can become "stuck in" loss and exist in a "dysfunctional state" (Conroy & O'Leary-Kelly, 2014: 74; Fraher & Gabriel, 2014; Obodaru, 2017). A recent study on workers adopting more portable and transient careers has suggested that, in these cases, being connected to institutions may help individuals manage transitory emotions such as anxiety and foster a sense of hope (Petriglieri, Petriglieri & Wood, forthcoming).

Organizations seeking to make changes to their identity may be able to manage change efforts to ease the emotional ramifications of identity change. Such efforts can involve the use of framing strategies to link past identities to new ones by using orienting values, devaluing the old identity or deploying emotional rhetorical strategies to manipulate organization members into new identification (Fiol, 2002; Moufahim, Reedy & Humphreys, 2015; Rao et al., 2003; Schultz & Hernes, 2013). One such emotional strategy, documented by Moufahim and colleagues (2015), is the use of "emotionality, the direct appeal to feelings of anxiety, anger, loss and vulnerable pride to draw their readers into its narrative." Organizations, thus, appear to be able to use the host of emotions triggered by identity threat to their advantage. However, if these emotions are not considered or managed, change efforts may be derailed by emotional reactions. This research highlights a more strategic take on emotions in identity dynamics.

### 2.3.3 Social Validation and Emotions

People do not operate in a vacuum; while actors can claim identities and enact them through their understanding of "the role behaviours that mark an identity in a given network" (Turner & Stets, 2005: 117), identities are negotiated between actors and thus require validation from others (Ibarra & Barbulescu, 2010; Petriglieri & Petriglieri, 2010; Swann, Johnson & Bosson, 2009). This need for a positive sense of self is not merely rooted in the cognitive, but it is also deeply affective (Brown, 1997; Driver, 2009) – it allows actors to feel good about themselves and their social positions. This form of social validation, sometimes called the identity verification process, provides feedback on whether a given actor is meeting the expectations tied to an identity (Stets & Trettevik, 2014: 36): "In identity theory, emotions appear based on identity performances and the extent to which individuals think that others see them as meeting the expectations tied to a particular identity in a situation." In general, it is understood that positive emotions come from identity validation and negative emotions arise from failed validation. The intensity of emotion felt in response to failed validation can vary depending on the relative closeness and power of the others who validate or fail to validate (Stets & Trettevik, 2014), or the salience or commitment the individual has to the identity. The greater "the commitment to an identity . . . the greater is the emotional potential in others' reactions to role performances [to mark] an identity" (Turner & Stets, 2005: 118). Actors can attribute the lack of verification to themselves or to others, which leads to embarrassment and shame or hostility and anger (Stets & Trettevik, 2014; Turner & Stets, 2005).

Validation is relevant at an organizational level as well. An organization's actions can produce positive emotions if they are identity-consistent, or negative emotions if they are not identity-consistent (Dutton & Dukerich, 1991). This can lead actors to try to remedy or repair actions or activities to realign with identity expectations. However, overt positive validation of an organization's identity from an external audience – while generally associated with positive emotions – can begin to generate negative emotions if those identified with this identity see the portrayal of the organization as inconsistent with what is going on internally (Kjærgaard, Morsing & Ravasi, 2011). Identity coherence is thus important at an organizational level too.

Social validation of claimed identities can trigger emotions; these emotions can then serve as the fuel that leads actors to change, alter or try on alternate identities (Ibarra, 1999). Accordingly, while "[o]nly recently in the history of identity have emotions been examined," the "insight that we have an emotional response to how we think others see us, and whether we think they see us as living up to or failing to live up to who we claim to be, has become important in understanding emotions in identity theory" (Stets & Trettevik, 2014: 33). Further research could examine the emotional implications of validation in contexts that reflect the realities of managing multiple identities (Besharov, 2014; Pratt & Corley, 2007).

Emotions underpin identity dynamics and theorizing through identification, transitions and validation. Yet much of the discussion around emotions has still been relatively implicit and people-centric. Recently, there have been calls in the literature to pay more explicit attention to the role emotions play (Cascón-Pereira & Hallier, 2012; Conroy & O'Leary-Kelly, 2014).

## 2.3.4 Directions for Future Research

In summary, emotions are important for identity and for forging identification with social groups, roles, organizations and communities. Once such identification has taken place, it can generate positive emotions, such as pride, but also trigger negative emotions if there are threats to the source of identification. Existing work in this area is in line with a people-centric perspective on the role of emotions in identity dynamics. Yet it has still been suggested that little work has "explor[ed] the emotional side of identification" (Pratt, 1998: 180) and "a wide range of important issues await further examination. These include, for example, the relevance of emotions for OI [organizational identification]" (He & Brown, 2013: 24). In fact, in addition to being an antecedent or an outcome of emotion, identification itself may be an emotional process (Carr, 1998, 2001).

Emotions also have been important in understanding reactions to identity transitions and in managing these changes. The importance of emotional regulation has been suggested at the individual level, but further systematic analysis is needed in relation to role-based, organizational and collective identity change, providing opportunities for future research. We also might consider how emotions impact the relevant validation or legitimacy of certain identities. Wry, Lounsbury and Glynn (2011) propose that a collective identity is likely to be legitimated when there are strong identity stories. To what extent might emotions impact the relative success or failure of such stories or narratives in garnering support for an identity?

Beyond the themes mentioned earlier, a few studies place emotions more centrally in their analyses (e.g., Giorgi, Guider & Bartunek, 2014; Giorgi & Palmisano, 2017; Howard-Grenville et al., 2013; Petriglieri et al., forthcoming). For example, Koerner (2014) identifies that courage can be a form of identity work, and Ainsworth and Hardy (2009) show that identity work can regulate emotions. Recent research has also revealed that emotional labor can strengthen identification with a role (Humphrey, Ashforth & Diefendorff, 2015), but that it also can lead to emotional taint – an emotional form of dirty work (McMurray & Ward, 2014; Rivera, 2015). In organizations, several papers argue, group-specific social or professional identities can be associated with distinct emotions that distinguish actors within the organization (Cascón-Pereira & Hallier, 2012; Coupland et al., 2008), and that these identities and their associated emotions can influence strategy implementation (Huy, 2011). In these findings, emotions are not just the by-products of identity processes "but also provided signals that helped them shape the eventual cognitive definitions, meaning and enactments of their identities" (Cascón-Pereira & Hallier, 2012: 140). Howard-Grenville and colleagues (2013) have shown the role emotions can play in helping resurrect a collective identity. Petriglieri et al. (forthcoming) take an exciting first step in studying emotions and identity dynamics in precarious work contexts, and they use a novel psychodynamic approach to do so, pointing to important avenues for future work. In fact, given the deeply personal experiences of identity dynamics, more utilization of psychodynamic theory would be valuable in enriching the depth of our understanding of identity and identity processes.

This research signals potential opportunities for future work to think about the ways in which emotions may structure, define or constrain identities. Overall, the identity literature has revealed important insights into the role of emotions as people-centric, but could expand beyond this into more structuralist views of emotion. A structuralist perspective would be consistent with work on identity that has focused on identity control and regulation (Alvesson & Willmott, 2002; Thompson & Willmott, 2016; Thornborrow & Brown, 2009). It also provides an avenue to engage with institutionalists' call to link identity and institutions (Besharov & Brickson, 2016; Glynn, 2008, 2017), but focusing on the emotions as a mechanism for this linkage.

Based on this overview, we can see that emotions have been actively considered in the identity literature within organizational and management theory. In many ways, the state of emotions in the identity literature is quite advanced when compared to other areas of organization theory, but as identity scholars have suggested, much room remains for further development on the role of emotions in identity dynamics (Conroy & O'Leary-Kelly, 2014; Pratt, 1998). If we evaluate this work in light of the three perspectives on the role of emotion, we can see that most of the work has been people-centered, with some work focusing on the more strategic use of emotion, and even less from a structuralist perspective. It also highlights potential opportunities for further examination in the literature. What might combining a strategic and structuralist perspective on emotions look like in the identity literature? For example, Thornburrow and Brown reveal the ways in which "preferred self-conceptions of men in an elite military unit were disciplined by the organizationally based discursive resources on which they drew" (2009: 355). To what extent might desired or adopted identities be shaped by emotional rules or registers, and how might other actors using these emotional rules influence identification processes if they manipulated or strategically deployed particular emotions? It is noteworthy that much of the research we have reviewed here conceptualizes emotions as linked to (as antecedents or outcomes) identities and identity processes. Yet the review implies a fruitful possibility of a more radical research orientation, whereby emotions are core to identities. It might be similarly interesting to connect a people-centric perspective with a structural one, exploring whether the feeling rules or registers associated with a given organization or profession shape people's responses to them. One way to do this is to consider contexts where there are clearly expressed feeling rules and registers (highly professional spheres) and study them in contrast to those contexts where feeling rules and registers are less well articulated, like in the precarious work environments that Petriglieri et al. (forthcoming) identify. We might also explore whether some identity-emotion combinations are more likely to trigger identification than others. What role might the presence of both positive and negative emotions have in generating emotional ambivalence, and how might this impact identification processes? In summary, within this broad literature, we see important links to emotions – but also identify exciting opportunities for future work.

## 2.4 Organizational Learning and Change

Organizational learning and change are both topics that have long been of interest to organizational theorists, and the two topics share an important preoccupation with the ways in which employees experience destabilization at work. This has made clear how "organizations are intensely emotional environments" (Clancy, Vince & Gabriel, 2012: 521) and revealed the implications of emotions for both learning and change initiatives. This common focus is why we review both of these literatures in the same section.

### *2.4.1 Organizational Learning*

Organizational learning is defined as "a change in the organization's knowledge that occurs as a function of experience," involving "changes in cognitions, routines and behaviors" (Argote, 2011: 440). Vince (2001: 1329) argues that organizational learning is "constructed from the interaction between emotion and power that creates the social and political context within which both learning and organizing can take place." Knowledge is power, and learning changes power positions (Vince, 2001). Like Vince, Sillince and Shipton (2013: 343) emphasize that organizational learning is "a collectively experienced emotional journey," yet too little attention has been paid to emotions in learning, and no integrative framework exists (see also Argote & Miron-Spektor, 2011; Crossan, Maurer & White, 2011; Fineman, 2003).

What existing work in this domain does reveal is that emotions are involved in the anticipation, the experience and the aftermath of organizational learning processes (Fineman, 2003). As Gabriel and Griffiths (2002: 215) argue:

Learning as part of an exciting group is different from learning in a group riven with rivalries and acrimony . . . It is not the case that cynical managers, acrimonious groups and defensive organizations discourage learning. Far from it. What they do is to encourage a kind of learning that promotes defensive attitudes, conservatism and destruction of all new ideas as potentially threatening and subversive.

In a comprehensive summary of emotions research in organizational learning, Sillince and Shipton (2013) categorize determinants of different types of emotions in organizational learning based on whether the situation was familiar or unfamiliar, and whether it validated or invalidated people's construct systems (or understandings of how things are and ought to be). Familiarity and validation were associated with comfort (calmness, relaxation), while familiarity and invalidation were associated with frustration. In unfamiliar learning situations, when people find aspects of the new knowledge or situation validating (i.e., they believe they can be successful, or that new, desired paths are open to them), they are likely to react with enthusiasm, excitement (Sillince & Shipton, 2013) and proactivity (Oreg et al., 2018). Such positive emotions are associated with more engagement, innovation and creativity (Rock, 2009; Rock & Tang, 2009). Yet, as Sillince and Shipton (2013) note, unfamiliar situations which invalidate the self (or threaten self-identity, Fineman, 2003) elicit unpleasant emotions like fear, anger and threat. As Vince (2001) has argued, organizing for organizational learning is fraught with both politics and emotions, and negative emotions are often avoided or covered over, reinforcing existing power relations, leading to cynicism and restricting organizational learning. When emotions are expressed, they are likely to be contagious among members sharing similar experiences (Bartunek, Balogun & Do, 2015).

These highly person-centered approaches to emotion dominate the literature on organizational learning, with limited work taking a more strategic perspective. More structural approaches to emotions in organizational learning are linked to research on routines and capabilities since learning is embedded within and takes place through routines and capabilities. Such work remains quite limited, however (Lilius et al., 2011). Grodal et al. (2015), for example, studies help-giving and help-seeking routines among high-tech workers, finding that both givers and seekers become emotionally engaged through combinations of cognitive and emotional moves that align or elevate their affective states. On the capability side, Lilius et al. (2011) examines compassion capabilities, which these authors argue influences organizational commitment, recovery from painful circumstances, absenteeism and productivity. They identify a number of relational practices that underpin compassion as a collective capability, including such things as acknowledging, celebrating, offering help and others, which together create high-quality connections between organizational members and the willingness to cross work/life boundaries to offer support.

### 2.4.2 Directions for Future Research: Organizational Learning

In summary, there is a well-developed literature focusing on organizational learning that takes a people-centered approach to emotions, but significant opportunities remain to develop more research that takes more strategic and structural approaches. For example, how can managers develop learning structures and environments that are validating and that create excitement among learners? Some firms, for example, have gamified their learning programs to make them more fun and exciting and to help them become more validating. According to Jane McGonigal, the game-designing author of *Reality Is Broken: Why Games Make Us Better and How They Can Change the World* (watch her highly engaging TED Talk called Gaming Can Make a Better World at www .ted.com/talks), games help us to feel "blissful productivity" and to experience "epic meaning" by presenting us with challenges that are at the limits of our ability – but not beyond them. Over time, gamers "level up," building their skills so that they can take on more difficult challenges, and they do so in collaborative ways, building a strong social fabric. Such excitement is not typically associated with organizational learning systems. Can organizations strategically adopt gaming principles and make workplaces more motivating? Can exciting, learning-based cultures be developed within organizations, and what impact would that have on performance? Investigating gamification is only one example of how organizational learning research could benefit from incorporating more strategic and structural approaches to learning to complement the people-centered approaches that currently dominate.

### 2.4.3 Organizational Change

There is considerable overlap in the organizational learning literature and the literature on organizational change, in no small part because organizational learning is often associated with significant change initiatives and vice versa. Like the learning literature, much of the literature associated with emotions in organizational change processes takes a people-centric perspective (Oreg, Vakola & Armenakis, 2011), often consistent with a psychodynamic or psychoanalytic view of "organizations as emotional cauldrons where fantasies, desires and passions lead a precarious co-existence with plans, calculations and the application of scientific thinking" (Craib, 1988: 110). Researchers adopting a psychoanalytic perspective have focused on discrete emotions such as disappointment (Clancy et al., 2012), anxiety (Vince, 2010), anger (Lindebaum & Gabriel, 2016), caution and blame (Vince & Saleem, 2004) in organizations, often identifying underlying power and political issues (Vince, 2001, 2002, 2006), and discussing their impact on organizational processes (Lindebaum & Gabriel, 2016; Clancy et al., 2012). For example, Clancy et al. (2012) discuss disappointment in organizations, which they argue is intimately connected to power relations through its connection to expectations. Disappointment can be seen as the failure of oneself, or the failure of the other, resulting in withdrawal or blame, and often tainting relationships between organizational members. While these discrete emotions may occur in the context of change, they may occur at other times as well.

Research beyond that adopting a psychoanalytic approach has shown that positive emotions are often associated with proactive change behaviors and favorable interpretations of the change process (Bartunek et al., 2011). Other research has similarly identified that employees can have positive emotional responses to organizational change, including commitment (Herscovitch & Meyer, 2002), support (Meyer et al., 2007) and readiness (Armenakis et al., 2007). More commonly, however, it seems that people experience organizational change as traumatic, involving anxiety, frustration and confusion (Vince, 2001; Griffiths et al., 2005), loss (Fineman, 2003), resistance (Ford et al., 2008), resentfulness by subordinates, defensiveness by superiors (Vince, 2001), cynicism (Stanley, Meyer & Topolnytsky, 2005), withdrawal (Martin, Jones & Callan, 2005) and hostility (Simpson & Marshall, 2010). Oreg et al. (2011) provide a helpful review of the literature on responses to organizational change. Oreg et al. (2018) argue that most literature focusing on organizational change considers only the valence of affect (positive or negative), and not the intensity of the affect people experienced (activation). Considering both emotional valence and activation, these authors suggest that four possible responses to change exist: change resistance (associated with stress, anger and being upset), change disengagement (associated with despair, sadness and feeling helpless), change acceptance (associated with calmness, relaxation and contentment) and change proactivity (associated with excitement and enthusiasm). Responses are influenced by goal congruence, goal relevance and coping potential (Oreg et al., 2018).

Some of the negative emotions organizational members feel during change processes may result from poor change management (Balogun et al., 2015), including trust violations, communication breakdowns and unfairness (Ford et al., 2008; Bartunek et al., 2011). An interesting longitudinal study of radical change implementation by Huy et al. (2014) reveals the connection between emotions, the legitimacy judgments of leaders and change implementation.

In their study, they find that the middle managers who were charged with implementing the radical change were continuously evaluating the legitimacy of the top management team that directed it. When middle managers judged the top management team as illegitimate, it caused "their emotions to boil over" and they staged "an open revolt that collectively rejected the authority of their bosses" (Huy et al., 2014: 1651). These authors argue that legitimacy judgments of people, which are based on instrumental, relational and moral grounds (Tost, 2011), can be highly emotion-laden, and can change rapidly, shifting the balance of organizational change efforts quite substantially and suddenly.

Continuing in this vein, Balogun et al. (2015) examine the responses of senior managers, arguing that they were simultaneously change managers and change recipients, both making sense and giving sense throughout the change. In their study, the leaders of a UK subsidiary of a European company initially went from having strongly positive feelings (excitement, pride, pleasure) about a change initiative when they felt they had a shared responsibility for it (time 1) and were succeeding in delivering it (time 2). Their feelings turned to strongly negative ones when they felt they were not valued and they no longer fit the organization (time 3). They went from working hard to implement the initiative in times 1 and 2 to resigning from the organization in time 3, despite their (successful) efforts being valued by the firm. These authors argue that firm leaders should not be reified as unitary actors (see also Kaplan, 2008), but should be understood to exist in different senior manager interpretive communities that actively make sense of change initiatives and their roles within them. Affective responses in these communities can have significant effects.

### 2.4.4 Directions for Future Research: Organizational Change

Like the learning literature, most of the literature on organizational change takes a person-centered approach to emotions. Implicit in the studies focusing on senior managers is the idea that leaders may take a strategic approach to managing emotions through organizational change processes, involving leaders' sensegiving to employees (e.g., Huy, 2002; Huy et al., 2014). Yet this strategic approach remains underdeveloped, and there is certainly an opportunity to develop more research that explicitly considers the strategic deployment and management of emotions in change processes.

By contrast, we were unable to identify research that took a structural perspective to emotions in organizational change processes. Taking a structural approach does have some significant promise as a future research direction. For example,

Michel (2014) argues that persons and organizations are mutually constituted, organizations shape how persons experience and engage with reality and persons in turn structure the organizations in which they work. In her study, bankers in organizations that saw the world in terms of separate entities experienced it as controllable, and their organizations changed episodically. Other bankers perceived the world as mutually constituted, and they were aware of flux and uniqueness, which enabled them to change continuously with client needs.

While Michel's study did not deal with emotions, it is easy to see how emotions, as structured in organizational practices, norms and worldviews, could have highly significant impacts on organizational change. Additional work is required that explores emotions from a structural perspective.

## 2.5 Organizational Culture, Power and Control

While the introduction of emotional labor by Hochschild (1975, 1979) triggered extensive work in organizational behavior (cf. Wharton, 2009), this work also played an important role in bringing attention to emotion in the study of organizational culture and on power and control. Given these similar influences, we review both organizational culture literature and power and control research that connects to emotions.

### 2.5.1 Organizational Culture

Organizational culture describes the beliefs, values, assumptions, conventions, rules and artefacts (Schein, 2004) that prevail as shared meanings within an organization. The literature on organizational culture has studied the ways in which these shared meaning systems shape organizational dynamics. Within this broad body of work, there has long been an acknowledgment that emotions are both a driver and a manifestation of culture (Hatch, 1993). That is, emotions can be both an implication and a core feature of culture. For instance, Van Maanen (1991) finds that Disneyland's culture, rather than being the "happiest place on earth," was one of monitoring and constant supervision; this culture generated feelings of mistrust between leaders and workers. Fehr and colleagues (2017: 361) outline how organizations can generate "collective gratitude" as a result of their initiatives and culture, and Grodal et al. (2015) highlighted how certain routines can result in emotional engagement. Organizational culture can have emotional implications. This work is largely people-centric as it focuses on the emotional reactions to culture.

In other cases, scholars have taken the lead from Hochschild's work and studied the emotional or affective cultures of organizations, and their effects on organizations and employees (i.e., Barsade & O'Neill, 2014; Huy, 1999;

Martin, Knopoff & Beckman, 1998; O'Neill & Rothbard, 2017; Parke & Seo, 2017). Some of this work has focused specifically on how to foster positive organizational cultures: how organizations can "create an emotional ecology where care and human connection are enabled or disabled" (i.e., Frost et al., 2000: 25; Lawrence & Maitlis, 2012; Pouthier, 2017; Rynes et al., 2012). Collectively, this work combines both a people-centric and a more structuralist view on emotions.

Reflecting a more strategic view of emotions, other work has highlighted how cultures can be designed strategically by managers and so can their emotional content. For example, Kunda (1995) describes how managers of a US high-tech firm attempted to design and impose a culture that normatively controlled its employees by inducing both emotional attachment and detachment and positive and negative emotional orientations to work and the organization. Hatch and Schultz (2017) find that leaders of the Carlsberg Group strategically mobilized the organization's culture and history to evoke feelings of authenticity among employees to support an organizational change. The change proceeded more easily because it was seen as consistent with the organizational culture and identity. In a related study, Hatch et al. (2015) examine a strategic shift in identity associated with the Carlsberg Group becoming more like a cost-focused, substantially centralized, efficiency-oriented consumer goods company. Cultural shifts

**Video 4** Organizational Identity and Culture (www.youtube.com/watch?v=bIXjGUYrDMc).

Rights held by Mary Jo Hatch, Majken Schultz and Anne-Marie Skov. Used with permission.

associated with this change impacted the emotions of the employees, particularly because the "old" culture was strongly associated with Carlsberg's heritage and passion for beer and brewing (See Video 4 for an Academy of Management Discoveries overview of the paper called Organizational Identity and Culture). Thus, strategic manipulations of culture and emotions may have intended and unintended effects.

### 2.5.2 Directions for Future Research: Organizational Culture

Since organizational culture is itself a social structure, studies in this tradition inevitably employ a structuralist approach. That said, we were surprised not to find more recent structuralist research on emotions and culture that more explicitly examines how emotions are constituted in and of cultures. Perhaps this oversight is connected to the larger challenges facing culture scholars. Has research on emotion and culture been cannibalized by the research agendas of identity scholars (Corley et al., 2006) and now institutionalists scholars (Hatch & Zilber, 2012)? We echo the call for others to revive studies of culture in organization theory (Hatch & Zilber, 2012). We are encouraged, however, that the organizational culture literature has combined structuralist approaches with both strategic and person-centered viewpoints. In fact, the combination of all three approaches fits more naturally in studies of organizational culture than in most of the other literatures in organization theory.

We also feel there is room for more culture research that casts emotions in a starring role rather than the usual supporting role they play. One direction could be hybrid organizations that combine two or more divergent affective cultures, as Battilana and Dorado (2010) find in a Bolivian microfinance organization. How are different cultural prescriptions regarding emotional feeling and display rules negotiated when members must interact with one another? How are value differences negotiated across subcultures, with their attendant moral emotions? More strategically, studies could examine if emotions embedded in culture are associated with different organizational outcomes. For example, are there specific emotional cultures that affect a) organizational resilience to environmental shocks? b) learning and adaptation? c) innovation? A range of such studies is possible.

### 2.5.3 Organizational Power and Control

Emotions have also been linked to power and control in organization theory (Hancock & Tyler, 2001; Fineman, 2004), with critical management scholars playing a crucial role in developing the connection between these concepts (for an overview, see Fotaki, Kenny & Vachhani, 2017). Indeed, cultural control via emotions and emotional labor (Hochschild, 1979) has been one of the earliest insights in the literature where emotions have been central to the theory. This work has found that emotional control and regulation can provide a tighter and deeper hold on employees than conventional bureaucratic mechanisms (Lindebaum, 2017; Van Maanen & Kunda, 1989). Work on emotions, power and control has spanned the structuralist, people-centered and strategic perspectives.

Structurally, organizational rituals and practices rely upon emotions (Durkheim, 1915; Collins, 2004; Summers-Effler, 2002) and so this body of work has examined the ways in which these emotions create and maintain systems of power. Research on subjectification (Foucault, 1977), for example, defined as how "power ... produces the kinds of people we feel we naturally are" (Fleming & Spicer, 2007: 23), has employed emotional and psychodynamic aspects to challenge the prior notion of subjectivity as permanently fixed (Clegg & Baumeler, 2010; Hamilton & McCabe, 2016). For example, in their studies of UK banks, Knights and McCabe (1998) and McCabe (2000, 2004) illustrate the way subjectification was observed to have a strong emotional aspect. This is because, as other power scholars have found (Fineman & Sturdy, 1999; Gabriel, 1999), subjectification entangles "the very heart of the employee" (Fleming & Spicer, 2014: 268) and "works through moments of feeling such as desiring recognition or fearing exclusion and alienation" (Kenny, 2012: 1188).

Beyond subjectification, scholars in this domain have also conceptualized emotion from a more strategic perspective (Pfeffer, 1981; Hardy & Clegg, 2006), where emotion acts as an organizational tool mobilized to defeat conflict and, thus, to maintain power over workers. Hochschild's (1979) early focus on emotions as controlled by management and organization and the resulting alienating effects has been continued by critical management scholars. Concepts such as emotion work, labor and regulation have been used to explain efforts by individuals or organizations to obey, control or resist the emotional rules (i.e., Fineman, 2000; Grant, 2013; Pierre & Robert, 2004). For example, Fleming's (2009) study of the managerial trend of authenticity highlights the nefarious aspects of emotional rules and their accompanying emotional labor and work. In this study, the rule to both display and feel "authentic" prompted conflict between worker desires for individuality and opaque organizational standards of employee behavior. The authenticity-related feeling and display rules entrenched managerial control by prompting a performance of an organizationally sanctioned personality or personal brand (Vallas & Cummins, 2015). In many ways, much of this work has pointed out that "when emotion management fails, so can the organization" (Fineman, 2000: 5).

Researchers have also depicted emotions strategically in other areas of power scholarship, while also considering how such actions prompt emotional responses, bringing together the strategic perspective with the people-centered perspective. For instance, Goss and colleagues (2011) examine how a UK organization mandated to support women who are subject to traditional forced marriages used "counter" power rituals to allow women to express "deviant emotions" and rescript power dynamics to allow themselves agency. Other studies have examined how people deploy humor strategically to resist organizational power (e.g., Rodrigues & Collinson, 1995).

Overall, within this literature there is disagreement on the extent to which emotional work and labor are conceptualized as a process of oppression and exploitation for the strategic purpose of organizational gain or a more neutral necessity that can have differential impacts on those enacting and engaging with emotions (Hochschild, 2011; Van Maanen, 1991; Elfenbein, 2007; Uy, Lin & Ilies, 2017; Williams, 2007). In their study of a supermarket, Endrissat, Islam and Noppeney (2015) attempt to address this tension and explore the ways in which emotional labor may simultaneously be both exploitative and valuable to those engaging in it. They find that individuals can find personal elements of value in the feeling rules that define and control their own actions.

### 2.5.4 Directions for Future Research: Organizational Power and Control

Like the culture literature, this literature adopts numerous perspectives on emotions, and we find this promising. Building on this work, we see some exciting opportunities for development.

We believe it is vital that scholars continue to integrate the consideration of emotions in studies of power and control. While much work in mainstream and critical scholarship has covered subject positions and experiences of emotions and power, physical bodies remain critically understudied from a sociological and anthropological viewpoint. This is potentially problematic since emotion implicates subjects, bodies and experiences. For critical scholars, we thus echo Fotaki et al.'s (2017) call for future research on emotions, power and embodiment, or the way of describing the visceral bodily experiences, in and with inhabited worlds. How do emotions and felt bodily experiences entangle with the production of cultural meanings? How are emotions and subjectification entangled with the production of power hierarchies, dynamics and systems of control? For example, many women have described coming forward to complain about sexual harassment by their managers and coworkers only to be shamed into silence by being made to believe it was their fault. How do these shaming processes work? How can they be avoided? We urge mainstream scholars to look beyond traditional functionalist notions of power and the strategic and people-centered perspectives of emotion that they naturally imply. For example, how might incorporating an understanding of power through the concept of subjectification change existing scholarship on emotions in identity theory or organizational culture? The link between power and emotions remains a rich area for future scholarship.

## 3 Theories Featuring More Limited Work on Emotions: Sensemaking, Practice Theory, Network Theory and Entrepreneurship

### 3.1 Sensemaking

Developed by Karl Weick in 1995, sensemaking has emerged as an influential and prolific research stream in both organization theory and organizational behavior. Bridging the work on social psychology and social constructionism, the perspective is particularly focused on understanding "the process through which individuals work to understand novel, unexpected, or confusing events" (Maitlis & Christianson, 2014: 58). People notice cues and interpret them, then act on their interpretations (Maitlis & Christianson, 2014; Heaphy, 2017), developing discursive accounts of their perceived reality (Maitlis, 2005). While some research focuses on sensemaking as a phenomenon with intrinsic interest, it has also been treated as an explanatory mechanism for other phenomena, including organization change processes (Bartunek et al., 2006; Gioia & Thomas, 1996), crisis management (Maitlis & Sonenshein, 2010; Weick, 1993), identity processes (Pratt, 2000; Pratt, Rockmann & Kaufmann, 2006) and strategizing (Plambeck & Weber, 2010; Rouleau, 2005). While researchers with this perspective have not studied emotions extensively – which has been a key criticism of this research stream (Maitlis, Vogus & Lawrence, 2013; Sandberg & Tsoukas, 2015) – emotions have been identified as important to this perspective. Some researchers have gone further by suggesting that emotions are not only important, but pervasive in sensemaking processes (Maitlis et al., 2013). In this section, we lay out key features and premises of the sensemaking perspective and then review the roles that emotions have played in prior research.

### *3.1.1 Key Features of Sensemaking*

As noted earlier, a unique aspect of sensemaking research is that it bridges social psychology and social constructionist social science – two research streams that do not typically mix. Sensemaking is a retrospective process (Weick, 1995) that is initiated by a person's encounter with the unexpected. The theory also diverges from social psychology, which tends to be grounded in realist ontology, whereby the world is seen as separate and independent from a particular person or organization, and the person's/organization's actions are meant merely to uncover and respond to the environmental stimuli. In contrast, Weick and other proponents of the sensemaking perspective have adopted the social constructionist premise that the world is not simply discovered and responded to but rather enacted through the actions of people and organizations (Smircich & Stubbart, 1985; Weick, 1979). In other words, people and organizations are active participants in the construction of the world they inhabit through their actions.

Sensemaking does not take place in isolation, and people's sensemaking efforts are influenced by others in important ways. Most notably, the idea of sensegiving acknowledges that influential others – such as leaders – can help guide people's sensemaking efforts (Gioia & Chittipeddi, 1991; Maitlis & Lawrence, 2007; Rouleau, 2005). Another mechanism that is related to and often precedes sensemaking is sensebreaking (Pratt, 2000), which involves actively destabilizing people's existing cognitive schemas and assumptions in order to encourage identity reconstruction. As well, collective sensemaking in organizations enables coordinated action (Stigliani & Ravasi, 2012; Weick, 1995).

### 3.1.2 Emotions in Sensemaking Research

Emotions have been under-researched in sensemaking. When sensemaking scholars have incorporated consideration of emotions, they have primarily taken a people-centered approach to emotions, concentrating on emotional responses. In an insightful review, Maitlis et al. (2013) not only synthesize extant research on emotion in sensemaking (which is still quite limited) but also identify the implicit and pervasive role of emotions in sensemaking that was not specified in prior studies. They identify the role of emotions in triggering sensemaking episodes and in the process of sensemaking itself. They also recognize emotions as reactions to the sensemaking process. The role of emotions, then, manifests primarily along the people-centered dimension, because the focus is on how emotions mediate human experience.

For instance, surprise is an emotional state that is particularly likely to trigger sensemaking, given the close association between encountering unexpected events and the need for sensemaking. With respect to the role of emotions in the sensemaking process itself, it is suggested that emotional ambivalence (e.g., hope mixed with doubt) may increase the quality of sensemaking by causing people to be more open to different perspectives (Vogus et al., 2014). For example, strategic decision-making may be improved when strategists experience ambivalence (Plambeck & Weber, 2009). As well, Heaphy (2017) find that mediators, incredulous about a particular case, discussed it with their peers, who helped them to develop alternative perspectives that enriched their sensemaking. In contrast, intense negative emotions, such as panic and anxiety, can overwhelm people (Cornelissen, Mantere & Vaara, 2014), interfering with their ability to engage in the effortful work of sensemaking (Maitlis & Sonenshein, 2010). Finally, emotions (positive or negative) color sensemaking processes in a manner that affects how people experience the outcomes of various organizational change efforts and interventions (e.g., Bartunek et al., 2006) or the extent to which they are able to move on after a failed project (Shepherd, Patzelt & Wolfe, 2011).

### 3.1.3 Directions for Future Research

Most sensemaking research has focused primarily on deliberate attempts to make sense in discrete and episodic situations, taking a largely cognitive approach. Sandberg and Tsoukas (2015) argue that emotions are a topic that is fundamentally conceptually challenging to the sensemaking perspective as a result: embodied, tacit and emotion-infused processes do not sit well with the literature's dominant emphasis on deliberate, intellectual and episodic processes.

We argue that the study of emotions can advance sensemaking in a number of ways. Most obvious is the move toward a more holistic, embodied and culturally embedded conceptualization of sensemaking that is ongoing and forward-looking, rather than purely retrospective. Emotions would become more salient with such a focus, because emotions are essential mediators of human connection to and engagement with the social world. An insight from the study of emotions is that people are motivated not only by surprises and disruptions that force them into a reactive mode but also by proactive and projective desires and passions that animate the search for meaning (Schabram & Maitlis, 2017). A person might, for instance, be trying to make sense of the rules and norms that govern a profession s/he wishes to enter by imagining her/himself practicing that profession (e.g., Obodaru, 2017). Desire then animates the search for meaning and sets up high expectations that, when unfulfilled, have significant emotional impacts that intensify sensemaking and associated enactment processes. In such a case, sensemaking would be a primarily forward-looking process that is grounded in the idealization of the profession and its connection to the desired self.

Another direction for future research is to study emotions as they are used strategically in sensemaking, sensegiving and sensebreaking processes. For example, Heaphy's (2017) study of patient advocates mediating among patients, family and staff in a hospital shows that emotions can be used strategically to influence other's sensemaking. She found that mediators' empathetic accounts, which showed cognitive and emotional appreciation of other's actions and motives, could be selectively drawn upon to help opposing parties empathetically understand each other. This suggests that a valuable future direction is to explore more the strategic role of emotions in sensemaking, especially in the context of interactive processes. Research in organizational change has taken this strategic management of emotions perspective, involving leaders' sensegiving to employees (e.g., Huy, 2002; Huy et al., 2014). Similarly, Tracey's (2016) study of persuasion found that "affective work" involving the strategic use of empathy and guilt was influential in converting people to a particular view of Christianity, though he did not use a sensemaking perspective. More direct attention to the strategic use of emotion in sensemaking processes is needed.

While sensemaking is less oriented to structural considerations, research could also be directed toward understanding how the emotional framing and structure of particular accounts could increase or decrease their resonance in collective sensemaking processes. Giorgi (2017) has written about resonance with respect to framing, and Hochschild (2016) has argued that a deep emotional story involving "good citizens" whose rewards are being taken by undeserving others is structured into American President Donald Trump's political sensegiving and consequent popularity with his supporters (see Box below). Focusing on the connection between sensemaking and institutions can also emphasize the structural perspective. While Weick has called sensemaking the "feedstock" of institutionalization (1995), it is also the case that sensemaking may be stimulated by institutions (Weber & Glynn, 2006), and as we discuss in the section on institutions and emotions, institutions condition emotional experiences.

Watch a short video on Donald Trump speaking about illegal immigrants and the audience response. https://youtu.be/lv_ORlXPBvg.

## 3.2 Practice Theory

Over the past two decades, there has been a "practice turn which has characterized much of organization theory (Schatzki, Knorr-Cetina & Savigny, 2001;

Whittington, 2006)" (Smets et al., 2017: 2). While practice theory has a rich history with varied traditions, a key element that connects the diverse work on practice is that it aims to "reground our study of organizational activities in terms of phenomena that are actually done, as they become evident in the here-and-now" (Miettinen, Samra-Fredericks & Yanow, 2009: 1309). No episode of activity is seen as self-contained, and distinctions between micro and macro, as reified levels, are rejected with the aim to transcend such distinctions (Miettinen et al., 2009: 6; Reckwitz, 2002; Smets et al., 2017). The study of practices thus involves examining "the patterns of relationships among human individuals and how such patterns are learned and made durable" while "consider[ing] the field in which practices are carried out" (Nicolini, 2009: 1406).

The implicit tie to the affective in practice theory resides within the sociological roots of the theory in Bourdieu's habitus and the work of other theorists, such as Heidegger, who had affective undertones in their theorizing (Nicolini, 2012; Smets et al., 2017). Thus, a structuralist approach to emotions is relevant. Yet practice theory has not elaborated or extended deeply the work on emotions, despite its focus on the micro-interactions and lived practice (Smets et al., 2017). Practice theory is based on the premise that we "need greater focus on the actions and interactions of people in organizations" (Jarzabkowski & Lê, 2017: 437), so the limited attention to emotions is somewhat surprising. Even in the community of practice literature, a subfield of practice theory that emerged in response to the overly cognitive focus on learning, emotions are often not central to analysis, although the potential for their inclusion is certainly present (Wenger, 1998; Thompson, 2005).

However, practice theory does link emotions with values – the wants, desires and ends of practices as well as sometimes the means (Nicolini, 2012). It is noteworthy that "becoming part of an existing practice thus involves learning how to act, how to speak (and what to say), but also how to feel, what to expect and what things mean . . . absorbing or being absorbed in, a practice also implies accepting certain norms of correctness (what is right and wrong) as well as certain ways of wanting and feeling" (Nicolini, 2012: 5). Thus, emotions are in some ways core to "lived practice."

In this way, a few studies have begun to suggest that practices can be defined by certain emotions (Rennstam & Ashcraft, 2014; Reckwitz, 2002; Samra-Fredericks, 2004). Reckwitz has said, for example, that "every practice contains a certain practice-specific emotionality (even if that means a high control of emotions)" (Reckwitz, 2002: 254). The practice of yoga is associated with serenity (see Figure 3), and the practice of nursing is infused with compassion (Van Wierengen, Groenewegen & Broese van Groenou, 2017), while the

**Figure 3** The practice of yoga is associated with serenity.

Photo Credit: Life Style Post, Gabriel Garcia Marengo, Flickr

practice of management and science are more associated with detached objectivity – the absence of emotional expression (Toubiana & Zietsma, 2017). "Wants and emotions thus do not belong to individuals but – in the form of knowledge – to practices" (Reckwitz, 2002: 254).

Indeed, outside the management literature, it has even been asked whether emotions may be a type of practice (Scheer, 2012). Because emotions are seen as connecting people to practice, these studies reflect a fairly structuralist perspective on emotions (though practice theory itself is not a structuralist theory). Yet despite these clear linkages and work that shows data rich with emotion (Llewellyn & Spence, 2009; Martin, 2003), emotions are rarely central to work in this domain.

A handful of exceptions remain that fit better with the strategic conceptualization of emotions. Jarzabkowski and Lê (2017: 433) show how humor was used in everyday work "to surface, bring attention to, and make communicable experience of paradox in the moment by drawing out some specific contradiction in their work." Work by Samra-Fredericks has shown how strategizing at work is made possible through talk-based interactions that include "speaking morals" through emotions (Samra-Fredericks, 2003: 143). She argues that "language/talk assists the assembly of emotional displays for 'moving' an audience; that is, persuading others while simultaneously speaking a rhetoric of rationality" (Samra-Fredericks, 2004: 1106). Specifically, her work highlights the ways in which emotion is embedded in discourse and talk, and the role it plays in communication and persuasion. This work closely aligns with other research on rhetoric and framing that emphasizes the strategic importance of making frames emotionally resonant (Goodwin & Jasper, 2006; Jasper, 2011; Tracey, 2016; Giorgi, 2017).

### 3.2.1 Directions for Future Research

Despite all of this, "capturing emotional expressiveness being 'done' there-and-then between organizational members as part of their everyday task-based activities . . . remains rare" (Samra-Fredericks, 2004: 1114). Scholars have called for future work bringing together emotions, identities and the practice lens (Smets et al., 2017; Glynn, 2017; Lok, Creed, DeJordy & Voronov, 2017). We suggest that this is a domain that is ready for an expanded understanding of emotions, given its theoretical roots and preference for ethnographic and qualitative methods. Surprisingly, when we consider the work in this field in light of the three perspectives on emotions, studies that explore emotions have tended to be from a structuralist or strategic viewpoint with a dearth of examples of the people-centric conception of emotion. Given the centrality of the lived experience to this perspective, that seems like an important gap.

Practice theory, thus, might benefit from diving deeper into a people-centric perspective of emotions and considering how practices generate and foster specific types of emotions. This could extend into the strategic or structural realm, by connecting emotional reactions to practices and their ability to be altered and/or changed. Also exciting to consider is whether certain sets of lived experiences are inherently more emotional than others (as some work has hinted), and whether this variation impacts the way people identify with, commit to and perform these practices. Does collective practice involving significant shared emotions increase solidarity and identification with a group and commitment to a practice, as would be predicted by interaction ritual theory (Collins, 2004)?

Work on practice-driven institutionalism (Smets et al., 2017), while clearly making progress in terms of highlighting the connection between institutions and practices, could also benefit from engaging with emotions. Might emotions be a component of all practices? Should the emotionality of distinct practices be considered and evaluated? Answering these questions would bring a deeper focus to both the structural and, perhaps, people-centric perspectives as we might examine how the emotional norms in certain practices impact the adoption and institutionalization of practices. Another interesting avenue of exploration is how the relational and social focus within the communities of practice literature (Thompson, 2005; Wenger, 1998) might benefit from investigating the emotional elements that tie actors together, and/or what emotions may foster learning and community development. Overall, we see a great deal of potential for further work at the intersection of practices and emotions.

## 3.3 Network Theory

Social network analysis appears in multiple disciplines. Because it focuses on social ties, it is inherently relational (Mische, 2011) and thus we would expect it to be affected by emotions, though much of the work in network theory focuses on structure and position rather than the content or nature of ties. While there is some question whether it is actually a theory rather than a methodology (Salancik, 1995), Borgatti and Halgin (2011: 1168) argue that "network theory refers to the mechanisms and processes that interact with network structures to yield certain outcomes for individuals and groups." These authors also describe a theory of networks that "refers to the processes that determine why networks have the structures they do," treating networks as the dependent variable. Network theory's agenda is to "explicate the connection between structure and outcome" (Borgatti & Halgin, 2011: 1172), such as the connection between network position (Burt, 1992) or tie strength (Granovetter, 1973) and non-redundant information. Two types of models exist: one treating ties as pipes for the flow of ideas and information, and one treating ties as social bonds for coordination and convergence (Borgatti & Halgin, 2011). Thus network research in management has been used to examine interorganizational alliances for coordination, innovation and knowledge transfer (Coviello, 2006; McDermott, Corredoira & Kruse, 2009; Uzzi, 1997), entrepreneurial networks for resource acquisition, trust and support, assistance with opportunity development and access to financing, markets and social capital (Goss, 2008; Hite & Hesterly, 2001; Larson, 1992; Semrau & Werner, 2014; Shane & Cable, 2002; Smith & Lohrke, 2008; Stam, Arzlanian & Elfring, 2014), and intraorganizational networks for leadership effectiveness (Balkundi & Kilduff, 2006), knowledge sharing (Tsai, 2002) and value creation (Tsai & Ghoshal, 1998), among others (Monaghan, Lavelle & Gunnigle, 2017).

The importance of emotions features prominently in Granovetter's (1973) seminal work on networks and embeddedness. He describes strong ties as comprising emotional intensity, intimacy, reciprocal services and time. Research on interorganizational networks identifies trust and friendship in close and repeated ties, embedding actors in normative relationships (Uzzi, 1997). Further, Dahlander and McFarland (2013) show that network ties persist when people reflect on the quality of their relationship, which is likely to be heavily influenced by emotions. Even in structural hole positions (positions between two or more otherwise unconnected actors, each of whom has different/complementary information, Burt, 1992), which are generally considered quite powerful, emotions may be quite relevant. Zhixing and Tsui (2007: 1) find that structural hole positions did not confer expected benefits in collectivist China because the control benefits of the position are "dissonant with the dominant spirit of cooperation."

While much work suggests that cultural norms, moral values and even happiness (Wang, Sutcliffe & Zeng, 2011) are transmitted through networks, Vaisey and Lizardo (2010) instead suggest that shared moral worldviews are the basis of the emotional connections that lead to network formation, rather than the other way around. While people often build their networks instrumentally in order to increase their valued professional contacts, when they do, they feel "dirty" relative to when they connect for help and emotional support (Casciaro, Gino & Kouchaki, 2014), though professional ties may also exhibit relational pluralism, delivering social and emotional support as well (Shipilov et al., 2014). Once in social networks, people pay more attention to and share more information from people belonging to their in-groups (Rudat & Budar, 2015), suggesting that the relationship goes both ways – networks and their members coevolve (Tasselli, Kilduff & Menges, 2015). These considerations of networks are both people-centered and structuralist, since they refer to how people experience relationships with their network ties and to how network structures and emotions are mutually constitutive.

While primarily occurring outside the management literature, some studies also show the strategic use of emotions in networks. For example, Bail (2012) showed how anti-Muslim fringe organizations displaying fear and anger were able to dominate discussions in the mass media despite not holding mainstream or widely held frames. The amplification of the emotional energy of their frame through the media then changed the mainstream discourse itself. These findings suggest that high emotional energy can be a resource to increase network centrality by attracting attention to a node's frame. In addition, other work in social movement literature emphasizes that emotions can play a key role in mobilizing networks of activists (Goodwin et al., 2001; Gould, 2009; Summers-Effler, 2010), and that emotions are key strategic tools in creating a collective identity for a social movement, uniting activists with diverse backgrounds, and enriching their own emotional responses to movement activities (Perugorria & Tejerina, 2013; Taylor, 2013). Strategic use of emotions may also carry a risk, however, since some emotional displays can alienate some audiences (Jasper, 2006; Bail, 2012). For example, social movements promoting veganism and calling attention to the inhumane treatment of animals often use intensely emotion-invoking films and pictures to get their messages across, but their efforts are often met with denial, stigmatism and ostracism by people raised and embedded in status quo beliefs about animals as food (Delmestri & Goodrick, 2017; see Box below).

This disturbing video, produced by PETA, uses emotion-evoking images of animal cruelty to build its network of supporters: www.youtube.com/watch?v=CKee_SPSbio. See Jarvis et al. (forthcoming) for a discussion of how animal rights activists manage their own emotions while recruiting and while going undercover to film such videos.

### 3.3.1 Directions for Future Research

Because of the relative paucity of research, there is significant opportunity to "warm up" network research in organization theory by attending to emotions. Research using people-centered and structuralist approaches together might examine the degree to which people feel embedded within networks depending on what emotions are dominant within the network, for example. Further, research could examine the implications such emotional embeddedness might have for the constraining effect of network norms, the information flows in the network or the ability to access other resources in the network. For example, do information and resources flow more freely in networks featuring mutual caring/affection vs. in a professional network dominated by feelings of duty or moral obligation? Are people more faithful to network norms in professional networks vs. friendship networks? How are disagreements handled in different kinds of networks? Questions could also focus on how people interact with those from other networks depending on emotional connections. Does liking and trusting someone from another network help you become less embedded in your own network norms and more willing to accept alternate network norms, as Fan and Zietsma (2017) identify across logics?

From a purely structuralist perspective, research might examine differences in the structure and properties of networks formed on the basis of mutual affection or shared moral feelings vs. those formed on the basis of common interests or for instrumental purposes. Do network structures really operate similarly regardless of content, or does the emotional basis of a network influence the basis of network centrality (and thus the power and influence of given individuals in the network), for example?

With respect to the strategic use of emotions, researchers could borrow insights from the social movement literature to ask questions such as whether strategic emotional framing or behavior changes the centrality of different actors over time within networks, or if it affects access to network resources. Such questions can be asked within intraorganizational networks, or focusing on an entrepreneur and his/her personal network, or within interorganizational networks. As demonstrated, network research is ripe for emotional theorizing from people-centered, structural and strategic perspectives.

## 3.4 Entrepreneurship

Entrepreneurship research focuses on the "discovery, evaluation, and exploitation of opportunities; and the set of individuals who discover, evaluate, and exploit them" (Shane & Venkataraman, 2000: 218). While it is less of a coherent theory than a phenomenon or topic within organization theory, it is of increasing interest to organizational scholars.

As Goss (2008: 120) has claimed, "entrepreneurialism is a deeply emotional activity." Emotions impact every stage of the entrepreneurship process (Baron, 2008). The majority of work on emotions in entrepreneurship has focused on people-centered approaches to emotion, exploring entrepreneurs' emotions as well as the ways in which emotions impact social interactions relevant to entrepreneurial processes. Least studied is work that takes a structuralist view, focusing on the contexts that create specific emotional environments for entrepreneurship. We review these three areas in what follows.

### 3.4.1 Entrepreneurs and Their Emotions

Emotions impact the motivation for, experience of and performance of entrepreneurship. Entrepreneurs feel passion and love for their businesses that motivate them to persist even when the going gets tough (Cardon et al., 2005; Cardon et al., 2009). Entrepreneurs may also be motivated by compassion (Miller et al., 2012) and emotional connections to communities, causes or people (Fauchart & Gruber, 2011; Qureshi, Kistruck & Bhatt, 2016). For example, opportunity exploitation is negatively affected by fear and positively affected by joy, anger (Welpe et al., 2012) and excitement (Foo, Sin & Yiong, 2006).

Reciprocally, engaging in entrepreneurship shapes and generates emotions. For example, entrepreneurial action and effort can induce passion (Gielnik et al., 2015), which then induces further entrepreneurial action (Cardon et al., 2009; Collewaert et al., 2016). Grief is associated with failure

(Shepherd et al., 2011) and affects learning (Shepherd, 2009). Positive emotions are most likely to be generated when the entrepreneur's self-concept is congruent with the entrepreneurial social identity (Murnieks, McMullen & Cardon, 2017). For example, one of us recently had a guest speaker who had both a successful catering business and a technology business that had yet to gain traction. The entrepreneur's self-concept was more congruent with the technology business, and he discussed trying to extricate himself from the catering business so he could truly focus on the technology business, about which he was more passionate.

### 3.4.2 Entrepreneurship and Emotions in Social Interaction

Emotions are also relevant to entrepreneurs' interactions with investors, employees, regulators and others. For example, the extent to which entrepreneurs express passion in their search for resources (Mitteness, Sudek & Cardon, 2012) has been found to elicit different reactions from different stakeholders (Breugst et al., 2012; Chen, Yao & Kotha, 2009). Jennings et al. (2015: 127), highlighting a more strategic and people-centered view of emotions, show that an "entrepreneur's exhibited emotion, use of linguistic and visual symbolic devices, and ability to achieve resonance with the identities of contributing actors" can generate positive emotions for all those involved that can enhance the creativity of entrepreneurship.

Beyond emotional expression, however, it is useful to think of relationships between actors. For example, affective relationships between entrepreneurs and investors positively impact their interactions, facilitating venture growth (Huang & Knight, 2017). Doern and Goss (2014) show how shame, humiliation and anger entrepreneurs experienced in their attempts to appease Russian government officials corroded their entrepreneurial motivation. Other work in this vein has found that emotions were heavily involved in processes of co-creation between arts entrepreneurs and both their customers (Elias et al., 2018) and their producing organizations (Montanari, Scapolan & Gianecchini, 2016).

Work on entrepreneurial networks emphasizes how trust and support (Larson, 1992; Shane & Cable, 2002) are important for social ties and the social capital associated with embeddedness in networks with various characteristics (Goss, 2008; Stam et al., 2014). Most network research in entrepreneurship points to the valued resources associated with network ties including assistance with opportunity recognition, social support and access to financing and markets. These resources are unlocked by positive emotions such as trust (Hite & Hesterly, 2001; Stam et al., 2014).

### 3.4.3 Emotions in Context: Organizations and Culture

Studies that have taken a more structuralist approach examine the role of emotions in the environments relevant to entrepreneurship. For example, research has identified socioemotional wealth in family firms, which is a stock of altruism, affect and understandings in social relationships forming the basis for identity, belongingness and family values. Preserving socioemotional wealth may be more important than financial performance for family firms when assessing risks (Gómez-Mejía et al. (2007). In social enterprises, which are susceptible to mission drift as they scale, André and Pache (2016) highlight the importance of embedding the entrepreneur's care ethics in organizational culture and identity.

More broadly, research suggests that specific emotional cultures at an organizational, environmental or institutional level may be more or less conducive to entrepreneurship. For example, work on cross-cultural, base-of-the-pyramid, gender-based and ethnic entrepreneurship considers the way emotions embedded in the institutional context affect entrepreneurship (McKague, Zietsma & Oliver, 2015; Tobias, Mair & Barbosa-Leiker, 2013). For example, Mair et al. (2012) describe how development workers appealed to village elders' norms of caring for the less fortunate to protect women who engaged with the market. On the other hand, Slade Shantz, Kistruck and Zietsma (2018) show how social-emotional obligations in Ghanaian villages constrained the pursuit of entrepreneurial opportunities and growth. Other work has shown that constraints to entrepreneurial capacity can be overcome with emotional interventions: supportive relationships with "known strangers" fostered entrepreneurship in a poor community in Argentina (Martí, Courpasson & Barbosa, 2013), and helped a social entrepreneur overcome the negative emotions of poverty (Martin de Holan et al., forthcoming). In this way, more structuralist approaches to emotions have proven fruitful in enriching the literature on entrepreneurship.

### 3.4.4 Directions for Future Research

A growing stream of research has focused on individual emotions and their effects on entrepreneurial action, particularly in the early stages (opportunity identification and startup) and late stages (exit) of the entrepreneurship process, with limited attention paid to the middle stages (Cardon et al., 2012). Opportunity to expand the people-centered approach to emotions may lie in this middle domain. Work on emotions in team-based entrepreneurial dynamics is just emerging (Cardon, Post & Forster,

2017), which is surprising given how important teams are to entrepreneurial activity (Jennings et al., 2015). We expect that future work could specify the types of emotions in relationships that might be more productive or destructive.

In terms of strategic research on emotions, one obvious area of opportunity is in cultural entrepreneurship, defined "as the process of storytelling that mediates between extant stocks of entrepreneurial resources and subsequent capital acquisition and wealth creation" (Lounsbury & Glynn, 2001: 545). While authors in this research tradition focus on cognitive elements and establishing a legitimate entrepreneurial identity (Wry et al., 2011), as Goss (2008) reminds us, stories are symbolic resources that convey emotions. Emotional stories are more apt to resonate with and inspire audiences, connecting them to the entrepreneurial identity (Weber et al., 2008) and even making evangelists of them (Massa et al., 2017). Drawing from social movement theory and its focus on the strategic use of emotions to mobilize activists could be useful. How can emotions be garnered to support cultural entrepreneurship? The strategic use of emotions is likely to be useful for social entrepreneurship as well. How might the "dramatic performances" found by Jennings and colleagues (2015) be relevant for activating emotions to achieve differing entrepreneurial outcomes?

We believe there are also substantial opportunities for entrepreneurship research that is more sensitive to structuralist perspectives on emotions (see also Shepherd, 2015). Entrepreneurship is embedded in networks, communities and ecosystems, with varying degrees of emotional intensity (Goss, 2008). These may impact the extent to which action in a given entrepreneurial venture is competitive or cooperative, or category conforming or more innovative. We have little research that can provide us with guidance on how particular emotional cultures may impact certain entrepreneurial initiatives. Further, we are just beginning to tap into the impact that entrepreneurs' embeddedness in normative communities can have on the type and quality of entrepreneurial action. Lack of attention to the emotions associated with embeddedness can lead to impoverished understandings of how clusters, entrepreneurial ecosystems and incubators add value, and to poor assumptions about how entrepreneurship "should" be stimulated to counter poverty in developing contexts. Thus, while entrepreneurship research has enriched our understanding of entrepreneurial emotions, much work remains to link the entrepreneur to the structures and contexts within which they are embedded and to examine their effects.

## 4 Theories Where Consideration of Emotions Is Nearly Absent: Organizational Economics, Economic Sociology and Embeddedness, Organizational Ecology, Categories and Resource Dependence Theory

### 4.1 Organizational Economics: Agency Theory and Transaction Cost Economics

Organizational economics approaches such as agency theory (Jensen & Meckling, 1976) and transaction cost economics (Williamson, 1975) take a rational approach to organizational and interorganizational phenomena, emphasizing "self-interest seeking with guile" (Williamson, 1993: 458). Even though transaction cost economics discusses trust as a means of governing relationships, they primarily treat trust non-emotionally, as predictability – something that can be "produced" with incentives and constraints (Williamson, 1993). "Trust . . . is a particular level of the subjective probability with which an agent assesses that another agent or group of agents will perform a particular action" (Gambetta, 1988: 217). Williamson concludes that trust is primarily calculative in business or professional relations, and that the idea of a nearly non-calculative trust should be reserved only for close personal relationships (Williamson, 1993), effectively setting emotion-oriented trust outside the scope of the theory, as other emotions have also been.

Organizational economists value the partialization of analysis, sharp assumptions and reliance on deductive reasoning, providing their theories with predictive power. Therefore, we do not expect the scope of these theories to expand to include emotions any time soon because scholars may be concerned about affecting their predictive ability. Nevertheless, consideration of emotions could clarify the theoretical boundaries surrounding organizational economics (Crook et al., 2013). It is interesting to consider what the emotional underpinnings of self-interest might be. Is self-interest a fear-based response? How might considerations such as these change how we think about this core assumption driving these theories? We can also ask under what conditions is self-interest seeking set aside to pursue cooperative or altruistic outcomes? What signals, structures or practices can be used to suppress self-interest seeking and enhance consideration of the sociality of human experience? It is likely that emotions would be implicated as more than aberrations in questions such as these. Studies could be designed using person-centered, strategic or structuralist approaches.

### 4.2 Economic Sociology and Embeddedness

A number of economic sociology scholars have challenged the idea that people are hyperrational self-interest seekers. Indeed, sociology of markets scholars argue "that social relationships between market actors solve market problems, such as agency costs (Fama & Jensen, 1983) and transaction costs (Williamson, 1985)" (Fligstein & Dauter, 2007: 109). Economic transactions are embedded in social structures (Granovetter, 1985; McKague et al., 2015), and social relations impact firms' economic outcomes (Uzzi, 1997), refuting asocial conceptions of markets (Biggart & Beamish, 2003). Yet economic sociologists have tended to exclude emotions from consideration. Once again, trust appears to be the exception. Trust in interorganizational relationships (with multilevel influences, Schilke & Cook, 2013) has been found to impact performance (e.g., Zaheer, McEvily & Perrone, 1998).

Further, economic activity can indeed be embedded in "sentiment and solidarity" (Zelizer, 2007: 1058), which opens up opportunities to explore the role of emotions further. A few studies have made some headway in this regard. For example, Weber et al. (2008) describes emotional aspects of the cultural code associated with the grass-fed beef market, including authenticity, naturalness, pureness and cleanliness and nurturing. These emotion-laden ideas were motivational not only for customers but also for the farmers who accepted lower than average returns in order to participate in grass-fed beef farming. Several studies have highlighted the relationship between social bonds and market activity. McKague et al. (2015) describe how creating social relationships of trust, loyalty and warmth in Bangladesh facilitated more equitable and efficient economic exchange, while Tobias et al. (2013) find that more effective markets reduced social conflicts in Rwanda. Slade Shantz et al. (2018) find that social bonds in Ghanaian villages may suppress innovative market activity.

Together, these studies show that emotions can affect market structures and the experience of people within markets, and that they can be used strategically to engineer such effects. While these studies merely scratch the surface of the effects of emotions in economic activity, they show the considerable promise of future research that delves deeper into these effects.

## 4.3 Organizational Ecology

Organizational ecology is a highly structural literature in organization theory that "aims to explain how social, economic, and political conditions affect the relative abundance and diversity of organizations and to account for their changing composition over time" (Baum & Amburgey, 2002: 304). This literature challenges the view that market adaptation comes from the intentional efforts of managers of individual organizations (Peli, 2009), suggesting instead that change occurs through processes of environmental selection, not adaptation. Researchers working in an organizational ecology framework have taken a predominantly quantitative focus, and the focus on environmental selection instead of managerial intention has meant that people-centered and strategic views of emotions are unlikely to be a part of ecological theorizing. Structuralist approaches to emotions have also been nearly absent in organizational ecology theories. Hiatt and Sine (2014) provide one exception: they examine the effect of violence and conflict on new venture failure in Columbia, finding that fear and uncertainty in that context reduces the survival benefits of planning for new ventures. In addition, work that includes a focus on identities is linked to emotions, though emotions are not explicitly theorized. For example, Carroll and Swaminathan (2000) study the US microbrewery market, finding that a collective producer identity (comprising selection conditions within the niche) involves emotional components including anti-mass-production sentiment and love for crafting, taste and tradition. Furthermore, work combining social movements and organizational ecology has shown how social movements can influence the way audiences evaluate market offerings with significant effects on selection pressures (Hiatt et al., 2009; Sine & Lee, 2009), and it is not hard to imagine how emotions could play a significant role in such work. For example, temperance movement activists used shaming of drunkards to help to change social norms (Hiatt et al., 2009). Yet, because of the quantitative nature of such studies, emotions have rarely explicitly been empirically operationalized in such studies, let alone theorized. Work such as this has been instrumental in stimulating work on categories, which takes a more cognitive perspective to examine the audience reactions to categories that underlie selection.

## 4.4 Categories

Research on categories and categorization processes, emerging from the literatures on organizational ecology and institutional theory, is an area of growing interest (Delmestri & Greenwood, 2016; Navis & Glynn, 2010; Vergne & Wry, 2014). While we see significant opportunities to integrate emotions into category research, little has been done to date. Literature in this tradition is based on the premise that "social objects are evaluated via legitimate categories" (Zuckerman, 1999: 1398), which convey cultural codes of belonging. "Audiences first determine which category an organization fits into, and then determine the degree to which it conforms" (Vergne & Wry, 2014: 63).

The category literature has deep cognitive roots (Porac et al., 1995; Wry, Lounsbury & Jennings, 2014) and, unsurprisingly, has not engaged deeply with emotions. Recently, a number of studies have linked categories to identity (Curchod et al., 2014; Glynn & Navis, 2013; Navis & Glynn, 2010; Wry et al., 2011; Wry et al., 2014) and stigma (Delmestri & Greenwood, 2016;

Vergne & Wry, 2014). While most of these accounts remain highly cognitive, they offer hints toward the possibility and even the necessity of including more emotions in the study of categories. We see potential most notably within two areas of this literature: category emergence and evaluations of category straddling.

Categories do not always exist a priori; they are often constructed or emerge, before becoming widely accepted and legitimate (Khaire & Wadhwani, 2010; Koçak, Hannan & Hsu, 2014; Lee, Hiatt & Lounsbury, 2017). To gain resonance and acceptance with audiences, categories may not just need to gain cognitive appeal and legitimacy but may gain traction through emotional appeal. Boghossian and David (2017) show hints of this when they discuss the emotional experience of pride that led to the emergence of artisanal Quebec Cheese. Further research can benefit from seeking to examine the success or failure of category emergence in relation to cognitive versus emotional resonance and appeal. For example, does our emotional response influence the way we categorize? Consider this question with the following example in mind (see Box below).

Does our emotional reaction to something affect the way we categorize it? The robot Sophia, granted citizenship by Saudi Arabia, was designed to express emotions because, as she says in the video clip: "I want to live and work with humans so I need to express emotions to understand humans and build trust with people." Will Sophia the robot's emotional expression help us to categorize her as a relational being, or will we categorize her (it) as machine first, and react with disgust and fear to her human-like qualities? (https://youtube/dMrX08PxUNY)

An additional area of research that holds promise is the examination of category straddling, or blended categories, which focuses on the conditions under which category straddling or blending may or may not be penalized due to audience reactions (Hsu, Koçak & Hannan, 2009; Paolella & Durand, 2016; Wry et al., 2014). If identity (with attendant emotional investments) can be wrapped up in a category (Curchod et al., 2014; Navis & Glynn, 2010), then category spanning or blending might provoke emotional reactions among actors who identify with one of the categories, but no emotional reactions among those with no such identity investments. In general, violators of category norms may provoke emotional reactions, since they would be seen as morally illegitimate (Hannan, Pólos & Carroll, 2007). Building on this idea, Ody-Brasier and Vermeulen (2014) hypothesize and find that Champagne grape sellers charged higher prices to those who violated the category's norms, suggesting that such violations triggered emotions such as irritation and indignation. This work suggests future research opportunities exploring the connection between emotions from people-centric and structuralist perspectives on emotions.

Despite these possibilities, the inherent cognitive underpinnings of categories research might lead scholars to suggest accounting for emotions to be ill advised or beyond the scope of the domain. Yet we suggest that introducing emotions to the category literature is in line with Glynn and Navis's call to attend to the cultural as well as the cognitive elements of categorization since, "although categories have structural properties as members of classification systems, it is their meanings – emotional, behavioural, social, or economic – that are likely to play the most important role in explaining organizations in terms of their identities and actions" (Glynn & Navis, 2013: 18). Thus, examining other possible ways emotions impact categorization processes seems a fruitful and exciting avenue for future research.

## 4.5 Resource Dependence Theory

Resource dependence theory (RDT) began with the notion that power and politics within and between organizations influence organizational survival. Introduced by Pfeffer and Salancik (1978), RDT views power and politics in an organization as determined by bargaining and exchange among participants in the organization and between organizational participants and stakeholders in the organization's environment. Yet, despite this focus on power, early work surprisingly left out emotions. Scholars drew upon the theory to derive largely supported hypotheses related to mergers and acquisitions, joint ventures and strategic alliances, interlocking directorates and executive succession (Hillman, Withers & Collins, 2009).

More recently, however, scholars have attempted to broaden the applicability of RDT by prompting a deeper consideration of the role of social contexts, relations and structures considering social embeddedness (Casciaro & Piskorski, 2005; Gulati, 1995; Gulati & Sytch, 2007). In addition, a few scholars theorizing in the context of family firms have engaged with emotion as a resource that shapes dependency relationships. Gómez-Mejía et al. (2007) and Berrone et al. (2010) have explicitly conceptualized "socioemotional wealth" as a resource, similar to other types of wealth. They thus invite "non-financial aspects of the firm that meet the family's affective needs, such as identity, the ability to exercise family influence, and the perpetuation of the family dynasty" into RDT considerations (Gómez-Mejía et al., 2007: 106). In their review piece, Davis and Cobb's (2010) recommendations for future directions are built upon the findings from the new social relations agenda within the theory, suggesting a role for emotions in the theory.

Thus, scholars interested in pursuing emotions-centered research in organization theory have a few toeholds in RDT. Looking to the future, involving emotions can provide new analytical dimensions to classic concepts in RDT, such as environments, enactment, effectiveness and connectedness. Originally, Pfeffer and Salancik (1978) conceptualized enactment of the environment very cognitively and focused on how and how easily organizations gather information, what organizations choose to focus their attention on and political support for certain information. Yet feeling and thinking are closely intertwined (Zajonc, 1980). Future scholars may consider how the emotional aspects of cognition could illuminate aspects of the enacted environment that were previously obscured by the cognition-heavy understanding of enactment. Resource dependence theory could examine how emotion-inducing factors could change the enactment of the environment. For example, the CEO of Dick's Sporting Goods responded emotionally to the activism of high school students for gun control after a horrific high school shooting in Florida. He stopped selling assault rifles and raised the age at which his customers could buy guns despite not being required to do so. "We have heard you," he said, showing he had changed the firm's focus of attention (www.bbc.com/news/world-us-canada-43223279).

To conclude, attention to emotions can do more than just improve how RDT scholars "talk about things" (Davis, 2015: 312), such as the conceptualization of additional "emotional" resources to be obtained. Consideration of emotions may reenergize RDT scholarship by tackling a new relevant set of phenomenon, such as the decision to change what an organization attends to based on emotional triggers. Emotions will allow scholars to look beyond "what we already know" about dependence management strategies and mechanisms (Davis, 2010, 2015). To paraphrase Davis and Cobb (2010: 26), "as long as power" and emotions "[play] a part in the conduct of organizational life, resource dependence theory will continue to provide insight," especially if enhanced by explicit consideration of emotions.

# 5 Conclusions

## 5.1 Closing Reflections: Where to from Here?

In our introduction, we argued that emotions play a fundamental role in social life that has often not been accounted for in organizational theorizing. As our review has demonstrated, emotions have substantial effects on, and are significantly involved in, most social processes and organizational dynamics, making this absence of theorizing concerning. We can see from the overview we have conducted that emotions act as fuel, providing the energy and the motivation for agency; act as glue, connecting people to social groups, social arrangements and social problems; and act as rust, slowing and stalling change as people's attachments can lead to defensiveness and the sense of being locked in to social structures (Zietsma & Toubiana, 2018). Emotions have, thus, positive and negative implications for a wide range of organizational processes. Yet, while there are a few reviews of the role emotions play in some core literatures (i.e., Lok et al., 2017; Goodwin & Jasper, 2006; Wharton, 2009), we have little that has provided a systematic overview of the role emotions do play across organization theory (as opposed to organizational behavior where such reviews exist: for example, Ashkanasy & Humphrey, 2011).

### 5.1.1 Looking at Emotions across Literatures

In this Element, we reviewed core organizational theories seeking to provide a more comprehensive account of how emotions are considered in organizational and management theory. We classified each theory according to the relative salience of emotions in the theory (from absent to strong) in each of the three approaches to emotions on which we focused in this Element (people-centered, strategic and/or structuralist approaches to emotions), identifying which approach was dominant in theories where there was sufficient emotion coverage. This allowed us to make sense of the diverse ways in which emotions are utilized in our theories and to develop future research directions that would help enhance and perhaps complicate existing coverage of emotions in these theories. Table 1 summarizes these assessments and Table 2 offers sample research questions that can be explored.

The emphasis on people-centered, structuralist and strategic approaches predictably varied with the ontological emphasis of the theory. Organizational culture, power and networks, for example, were strong or dominant in structural approaches, consistent with their more structuralist ontologies. For organizational learning, change, sensemaking, identity and entrepreneurship literatures, people-centered approaches dominated. In social movement theory, there was a dominant strategic perspective, which is fitting given the focus of this theory. Surprisingly, institutional theory, which one might expect to have a dominant structuralist approach, has had more work emerge from the strategic and people-centric perspectives. This is likely due to the current preoccupations with strategic agency (e.g., institutional work) and the person-centered experience of institutions (inhabited institutionalism) that the emotions agenda emerged from within institutional theory (Lok et al., 2017; Zietsma & Toubiana, 2018). However, despite these preoccupations, recently the structuralist approach has become more

**Table 1** Organizational Theories and Their Approaches to Emotions

| Theory | People-Centered | Structuralist | Strategic |
|---|---|---|---|
| | Focus on individual or collective emotional responses. | Focus on how emotions constitute, and are constituted by, social structures | Focus on the use of emotions as tools to affect others |
| Institutional Theory | Strong | Limited | Dominant |
| Social Movement Theory | Strong | Somewhat Limited | Dominant |
| Identity Theory | Dominant | Limited | Limited |
| Organizational Learning and Change | Dominant – Learning | Limited – Learning | Limited – Learning |
| | Dominant – Change | Limited – Change | Limited – Change |
| Organizational Culture, Power and Control | Strong – Culture | Strong – Culture | Limited – Culture |
| | Strong – Power | Dominant – Power | Limited – Power |
| Sensemaking | Dominant | Absent | Limited |
| Practice Theory | Limited | Limited | Limited |
| Network Theory | Limited | Dominant but limited | Limited |
| Entrepreneurship | Dominant | Limited | Limited |
| Organizational Economics | Absent | Nearly Absent | Nearly Absent |
| Economic Sociology | Nearly Absent | Limited | Nearly Absent |
| Organizational Ecology | Absent | Nearly Absent | Absent |
| Categories | Nearly Absent | Nearly Absent | Nearly Absent |
| Resource Dependence | Absent | Nearly Absent | Absent |

**Table 2** Sample Research Questions To Be Explored in Each Theory

| Theory | Research Questions |
|---|---|
| Institutional Theory | How do actors become emotionally competent in given institutional environments? |
| | How does the moral-emotive character (ethos) of an institutional order affect the experience of different configurations of institutional complexity? |
| | How can emotions be used to affect embedding and disembedding to enable people from different logics to work together? |
| Social Movement Theory | How do different framing strategies used by a movement impact its emotional resonance with members and activists? |
| | How does identification with and emotional attachment to a movement influence one's reflexivity and agency related to movement issues? |
| | How are social movements structured or shaped by emotional registers, feeling rules or emotional cultures? What impact does this have on movement success? |
| | How do movements use emotions to influence audiences in an online/big data/artificial intelligence era? |
| Identity Theory | How might an actor's emotional response to organizational identity threats influence said actor's other identifications? |
| | In what ways do emotions define identities? How do they structure identification? |
| | How might the manipulation or strategic deployment of particular emotions influence identification processes? |
| | How do emotions influence or shape de-identification or dis-identification processes? |
| Organizational Learning and Change | How might emotional investment influence an actor's responses to learning opportunities and change programs? |
| | How do institutionalized emotions or emotional cultures influence organizational learning and change? |
| | What is the impact of gamification on learning and change and what role do emotions play? |
| | Are particular emotions or emotional sets more or less helpful for fostering learning or change? |
| | How are emotions strategically embedded in cultures to affect organizational outcomes? |

**Table 2** (cont.)

| Theory | Research Questions |
| --- | --- |
| Organizational Culture, Power and Control | How does the visceral experience of discipline turn to anger for some and shame for others? |
| | How are emotions and bodily experiences entangled with the production of power hierarchies? |
| | How is emotion used strategically to subjectify others? |
| | Does the experience of specific emotional cultures lead to better learning, adaptation or resilience? |
| Sensemaking | How do emotional reactions to sensebreaking activities impact and shape subsequent sensemaking processes? |
| | How does the emotional content of social structures affect sensemaking, sensebreaking and sensegiving? |
| | How are emotions used to break down existing meanings in sensebreaking? How might these emotions be strategically managed to improve this process? |
| Practice Theory | How do specific practices foster specific emotions for those enacting them? |
| | How can emotions help to institutionalize practices? |
| | Can practice adherence or practice innovation be affected by tying practices to specific emotions? |
| | In what ways are practices defined by emotional registers or rules? Can changing this emotional content alter the nature of a practice? |
| Network Theory | In what ways do emotions affect the experience of embeddedness? |
| | How are networks shaped by institutionalized feeling rules or emotional registers? |
| | Does strategic emotional framing change the centrality of actors or affect network access? |
| Entrepreneurship | What emotions are most productive during business growth phases of entrepreneurial action? |
| | How do existing emotional cultures impact entrepreneurial action and the nature of entrepreneurial relationships in different contexts? |
| | How can emotions be evoked to achieve differing entrepreneurial outcomes? |

**Table 2** (cont.)

| Theory | Research Questions |
| --- | --- |
| Organizational Economics | What are the emotional underpinnings of self-interest seeking?<br>What social structures trigger relational emotions (such as trust or compassion) and suppress opportunism?<br>What signals, structures or practices can be used to suppress opportunism and highlight sociality? |
| Economic Sociology | How do certain emotional experiences affect various types of market activity?<br>How are markets and their cultural codes constituted by emotions? To what effect?<br>How can market makers manipulate emotions to drive market activity? |
| Organizational Ecology | How do changes in emotional climates influence selection mechanisms?<br>How are emotions structured into niche identities?<br>How do emotions in niche identities influence selection mechanisms and niche growth? |
| Categorization | How do people's emotional responses to category violations influence their actions?<br>How do emotions become structured into categories? In what ways can the emotional underpinnings of categories affect category identification and acceptance?<br>How can people's emotional reactions to categories be used or manipulated by market actors? |
| Resource Dependence | How does emotional attachment affect perceptions of resource dependence?<br>In what ways can socioemotional structures affect how resource dependence is perceived and enacted?<br>How can emotions be used strategically to manipulate perceptions of resource dependence? |

attended to in the theory (i.e., Friedland, 2018). Institutional theory thus may be quickly moving to a relatively balanced coverage of these perspectives. We see promise for this theory and others where there is not just balance across perspectives but also the combination of these perspectives. For example, Fan and Zietsma (2017), Massa et al. (2017) and Wright et al. (2017) have combined people-centered, strategic and structuralist perspectives, providing rich understandings of the full import of emotions in social processes. While many of the literatures feature a few studies that combine two or three of the approaches to emotions, these combinations offer substantial benefits for theorizing and the opportunity to make more explicit the role of emotions. We believe that most of the literatures could benefit from more research attention to such combinations, with resultant benefits for more sophisticated theorizing about emotions.

The literatures in which emotions were nearly absent include the literatures with the most rational and positivist ontologies: organizational economics theories, including agency theory and transaction cost theory, and resource dependence. While some of these theories arose in reaction to concerns about hyperrationality in economics, emotions may be too far from these theories' ontological roots to play a central role in these theories. Yet we see some opportunities to enrich these theoretical areas with emotions. For example, emotions and social connections are likely to mitigate concerns about opportunism, provide alternatives to rigid governance structures and influence the resource dependencies that actors will choose to focus on and enact. It may be precisely the *lack* of attention to social processes, including emotions, that makes these theories susceptible to being cast as "bad management theories" that destroy "good management practices," according to Ghoshal (2005: 75). Ghoshal argues that these theories, by propagating amoral worldviews among business students and managers, release managers from moral responsibility, and thereby create the conditions for *im*moral actions by managers. Perhaps if management theorists focused more on social and emotional connections among people and the organizations they inhabit and direct, we could make such connections more salient for managers and curb some of the everyday corruptions and opportunistic behaviors that are rampant in business.

Furthermore, we suggest that in at least two of the theories where emotions were absent, categories and economy sociology, the potential to truly understand the theories' focal phenomenon is substantially impoverished without consideration of emotions. Markets are built through human connections, and categories emerge and grow through the passions and identification of their founders, their early adherents and often their social movement proponents (see, for example, Massa et al., 2017; Sine & Lee, 2009; Weber et al., 2008). In fact, a rereading of some papers that have focused on categories and markets suggests that emotions are already there – in the data – though they have been left unacknowledged theoretically (see, for example, Delmestri & Greenwood, 2016; Ody-Brasier & Vermeulen, 2014). Weik (forthcoming) argues that without attention to affect, beauty and values, what she calls the "Weird Sisters in institutional analysis," we fail to truly understand motivation and agency. What new questions could be asked, and new processes understood, if we allowed emotions into the limelight?

While people-centered approaches are, and have been, valuable for bringing attention to emotions across all organizational theories, we suggest that we may have reached the limits of its insights in our scholarship. Deep consideration and integration of emotions to organization theory require emotional theorizing to move beyond examinations of emotions as mere reactions to organizational and social processes. As we argued in our opening section, psychological approaches that focus on autonomous individuals and intrasubjective experiences of emotions are not consistent with most organization theories. A more sociological approach to emotions that acknowledges their intersubjective, collective, relational and culturally structured nature is more ontologically consistent with the canon of organization theory. Thus, we urge researchers to give more attention to structural and strategic approaches to emotions across the literatures in organization theory. This means moving up a level of analysis in some cases and not merely considering emotions in individuals, but also their import in organizations, movements, fields and institutions.

When we embarked on this project, we had expected emotions to be absent in many of our theories of organizations. However, upon diving deeper into these literatures we were pleasantly surprised at the degree to which emotions have been considered (as we elaborate on earlier in this Element). While in the worst cases, emotions appear clearly in the empirical data but are never explicitly mentioned in the analysis, there are also many cases where emotions were explicitly mentioned in theorizing. Yet, often, this inclusion was sporadic and unsystematic – meaning you could find emotions "here" and "there" within the theories, accompanying other processes and constructs that have been more explicitly theorized, but not deeply theorized themselves. As a result, while emotions are referenced frequently in some domains, they are usually not part of a coherent agenda on the study of emotions or an elaboration of the emotional underpinnings or mechanisms relevant to the theory. What was missing from most literatures was explicit theorizing of emotions as constructs central to the core mechanisms of or arguments within the theory. We reject the notion that this is because emotions are simply not core to the theory – emotions are central to social life, and thus their absence in social theorizing is suspect! Can collective insights from existing studies on emotions help in the design of such a theory, rather than simply considering emotions as add-ons or components of existing theories? We believe our work on this project suggests that such insights are possible and crucial to further theoretical development.

Scholars have asked, "where are the new theories of organizations" (Suddaby, Hardy & Huy, 2011: 236)? We propose that one of the answers to this question is that it is time to advance an *organization theory of emotions*. The psychological orthodoxy that has permeated micro-theories of organizational behavior has even shaped the understanding of the micro-foundations of some macro-organizational theories and their assumption that the individual is the basic location of emotions. However, people spend their entire lives in organizations of some sort – whether work, family or community organizations. As a result, we would suggest that virtually all emotional experiences are fundamentally influenced, shaped or made meaningful by organizations. In other words, organizations are integral to emotions! Thus, while we have argued throughout this Element that organizational scholars need insights about emotions to enhance the power of their theories, organizational theorists also are uniquely positioned to advance the view of emotions as organizational phenomena.

### 5.1.2 Methodological Considerations

If we do indeed take the sociological view of emotions and bring them more explicitly into organization theory, how can we study them in a way that is sensitive to social structures, intersubjectivity, relationality and collective experience? As Fineman (2006: 688) explained, "[a] broad unravelling of the methodological canvass reveals emotions susceptible to exploration in many different ways, such as contextualized observations, ethnographies, free-form diaries, memory work, action research and phenomenological analysis … Clearly, the way we conceptualize emotion … provide[s] different vantage points on knowing emotions." How we study emotions is going to play an important role in the ways in which we can build a strong organization theory agenda for emotions.

Many studies have examined emotions in texts, including interview texts (Gill & Burrow, 2018), archival documents (Moisander et al., 2016) and social media data (Toubiana & Zietsma, 2017). In an age of "big data," this continues to seem like an appropriate way to study emotions. Social media data in particular seem promising because emotionality is so evident in the data, while also providing empirical opportunity to trace interactions and amplification. Yet, while the possibility of machine-coding voluminous social media data is tantalizing, it comes with risks, as emotional expression may use sarcasm or contain nuance that machine coding misses. For example, the statement "you deny me HOPE, how dare you!!!" was coded using Linguistic Inquiry and Word Count software (LIWC) as hope, when contextualized hand coding more accurately identified it as an expression of anger (Toubiana & Zietsma,

2017). We expect that as machine-coding techniques for managing big data are refined, new opportunities will arise for such analysis, and we encourage these to be considered with excitement and caution.

Lord, Dinh and Hoffman (2015: 278) argue that phenomena like emotions must be observed over time, as they continually evolve, and in context, since "like a computer monitor that is turned off, features are not activated when a concept, attitude, emotion, trait, group climate or organizational process is divorced from context." Thus, while we can examine emotions in talk and text, unless we are also examining their enactment, and connection to place and materiality in multimodal approaches, we can miss significant aspects of social life. Zilber (2017) urges us to consider seriously that meaning is made, and social events and arrangements are constructed, through combinations of discourse, bodily experience, emotions, visuals, material forms and place. While in social media, text and visuals may be the only data, in most social interactions, we have a much richer set of data from which to draw. Liu and Maitlis (2014) provide an interesting example of how to capture emotions in this way: they use video to capture both the textual and bodily expression of emotion as they engage in organizational processes (i.e., hand waving, smiles, laughs and winks, as well as tone and voice expression). Ethnographic data in general have very strong potential to reveal collective, relational and intersubjective processes in rich ways (see, e.g., Ruebottom & Auster, 2018). In particular, issues such as the relational nature of emotions, emotional energy, emotional contagion and amplification are challenging to study empirically, but may be more amenable to ethnographic observation, supplemented by interviews. Yet even ethnographic observations can be the basis of weak multimodal approaches, as Zilber (2017) illustrated; therefore rigorous efforts at coding are still required.

Perhaps unsurprisingly, the organizational theories that have attended to emotions most extensively to date have been the theories that are most open to qualitative methodologies. These methodologies have provided an opportunity to engage more deeply with the lived experience of organizations on the ground, where emotions can be hard to ignore. While qualitative methods will continue to be extremely valuable in developing emotions research, we cannot disregard the possibilities of quantitative methods. Harmon's (forthcoming) paper contributes to research on the cognitive and emotional microfoundations of institutions by studying the emotional tone of speeches and analyzing his data quantitatively. As we come to view emotions as more central to organizational theories, developing and enhancing quantitative techniques to measure these emotions is an important part of the research agenda.

### 5.1.3 Final Thoughts

Our review has shown that emotions are integral to social life and, thus, to organization theory. Yet emotions remain unrecognized in much organizational research, and are undertheorized even when they are recognized. Emotions are an integral part of fulfilling lives. By failing to recognize them or pretending they do not exist or are not theoretically relevant, we are impoverishing our theory. If, as Ghoshal (2005) has suggested, our models help to create the world we study, we are impoverishing our world and the lives of those we touch. What topics become unthinkable, what ideas become undiscussable, what experiences become unbearable when we do not enable the discussion of emotions? What possibilities might emerge if we allow our theories to reflect actors as emotional beings and organizations and other social structures as emotion-infused spaces and constructs? Importantly, as we reflect on what role emotions should play in the future of organization theory, we might take the time to reconnect to our changing social world. To understand this world fully, we need to understand the emotions that permeate it.

In news stories that were prevalent in early 2018, it was revealed that Cambridge Analytica, funded by right-wing political interests, used data analytics to analyze people's Facebook likes. This analysis enabled them to make arguably very accurate predictions about individuals' profiles, including their political and social affinities. While the full story has not yet emerged at the time of writing, it appears that these profiles were used to serve people stories that manipulated their emotions to influence their perceptions with respect to both the 2016 Brexit campaign and the 2016 American election of Donald Trump. In addition, Russian operatives stand accused of using bot postings on social media to polarize Americans' emotions, contributing to social disruption and conflict. In a recent ethnography of Tea Party supporters in rural Louisiana, Hochschild (2016) argues that public appeals to an emotional "deep story" of being "left behind" were responsible for the overwhelming support her participants gave to Donald Trump and the Republican Party. Their support was despite the fact that many of the party's policies were arguably contrary to her participants' economic interests, well-being and often prior environmental activism. This same emotional narrative has been identified as a part of the rise of populist leaders, and the decay of democracy, in many jurisdictions globally. The role of emotions in these major worldwide events is clear.

At the same time, the #MeToo movement around sexual harassment has revealed the toxic cultures of many organizations and industries that have created emotional wreckage around them. The globalization of opaque supply chains has enabled worker exploitation up to and beyond conditions of modern slavery, leading to disasters like the Rana Plaza fire in Bangladesh that killed more than 1,100 workers (Crane, 2013). Increases in inequality globally have shown just how ruthless unfettered capitalism can be. Work in positive organizational scholarship suggests it does not have to be this way: compassionate workplaces may have performance advantages, and people thrive when they can meaningfully connect with their work.

By ignoring emotions in our scholarship, we prevent ourselves from finding ways to mobilize positive emotions and dampen negative ones. For example, if populism is fueled by hate, to quell it we need to understand both hate and how we can foster other emotions to negate it. Failing to theorize emotions paralyzes and undermines our ability to understand what is driving people to act, and prevents us from fully being able to study and impact the grand challenges our world is facing.

We invite you, dear reader, to enrich your scholarship, your life and our world by fully attending to emotions.

# References

Ainsworth, S. & Hardy, C. (2009). Mind over body: Physical and psychotherapeutic discourses and the regulation of the older worker. *Human Relations*, 62, 1199–1229.

Alvesson, M. & Willmott, H. (2002). Identity regulation as organizational control: Producing the appropriate individual. *Journal of Management Studies*, 39, 619–44.

André, K. & Pache, A. C. (2016). From caring entrepreneur to caring enterprise: Addressing the ethical challenges of scaling up social enterprises. *Journal of Business Ethics*, 133(4), 659–75.

Argote, L. (2011). Organizational learning research: Past, present and future. *Management Learning*, 42(4), 439–46.

Argote, L. & Miron-Spektor, E. (2011). Organizational learning: From experience to knowledge. *Organization Science*, 22(5), 1123–37.

Armenakis, A. A., Bernerth, J. B., Pitts, J. P. & Walker, H. J. (2007). Organizational change recipients' beliefs scale: Development of an assessment instrument. *Journal of Applied Behavioral Science*, 43(4), 481–505.

Ashforth, B. E. (2001). *Role Transition in Organizational Life: An Identity-Based Perspective*, Mahwah, NJ: Lawrence Erlbaum Associates.

Ashforth, B. E. & Kreiner, G. E. (2014). Contextualizing dirty work: The neglected role of cultural, historical, and demographic context. *Journal of Management & Organization*, 20(4), 423–40.

Ashkanasy, N. M. & Dorris, A. D. (2017). Emotions in the workplace. *Annual Review of Organizational Psychology and Organizational Behavior*, 4, 67–90.

Bail, C. A. (2012). The fringe effect: Civil society organizations and the evolution of media discourse about Islam since the September 11th attacks. *American Sociological Review*, 77(6), 855–79.

Balkundi, P. & Kilduff, M. (2006). The ties that lead: A social network approach to leadership. *Leadership Quarterly*, 17, 419–39.

Balogun, J., Bartunek, J. M. & Do, B. (2015). Senior managers' sensemaking and responses to strategic change. *Organization Science*, 26(4), 960–79.

Barnard, C. I. (1938). *The Functions of the Executive*, Cambridge, MA: Harvard University Press.

Baron, R. A. (2008). The role of affect in the entrepreneurial process. *Academy of Management Review*, 33(2), 328–40.

Barsade, S. G. (2002). The ripple effect: Emotional contagion and its influence on group behavior. *Administrative Science Quarterly*, 47(4), 644–75.

Barsade, S. G. & O'Neill, O. A. (2014). What's love got to do with it? A longitudinal study of the culture of companionate love and employee and client outcomes in a long-term care setting. *Administrative Science Quarterly*, 59(4), 551–98.

Bartunek, J. M., Balogun, J. & Do, B. (2011). Considering planned change anew: Stretching large group interventions strategically, emotionally, and meaningfully. *Academy of Management Annals*, 5(1), 1–52.

Bartunek, J. M., Rousseau, D. M., Rudolph, J. W., DePalma, J. A. (2006). On the receiving end: Sensemaking, Emotion, and Assessments of an Organizational Change Initiated by Others. *Journal of Applied Behavioral Science*, 42, 182–206.

Baum, J. & Amburgey, T. L. (2002). Organizational ecology. In J. Baum, ed., *Companion to Organizations*. Blackwell: Oxford University Press, 304–36.

Benford, R. D. (1997). An insider's critique of the social movement framing perspective. *Sociological Inquiry*, 67, 409–30.

Benford, R. D. & Snow, D. A. (2000). Framing processes and social movements: An overview and assessment. *Annual Review of Sociology*, 26, 611–39.

Benski, T. & Langman, L. (2013). The effects of affects: The place of emotions in the mobilizations of 2011. *Current Sociology*, 61, 525–40.

Bergstrand, K. (2014). The mobilizing power of grievances: Applying loss aversion and omission bias to social movements. *Mobilization: An International Quarterly*, 19, 123–42.

Bericat, E. (2016). The sociology of emotions: Four decades of progress. *Current Sociology*, 64(3), 491–513.

Bernstein, M. (1997). Celebration and suppression: The strategic uses of identity by the lesbian and gay movement. *American Journal of Sociology*, 103, 531–65.

Berntzen, L. E. & Sandberg, S. (2014). The collective nature of lone wolf terrorism: Anders Behring Breivik and the anti-Islamic social movement. *Terrorism and Political Violence*, 26, 759–79.

Berrone, P., Cruz, C., Gómez-Mejía, L. R. & Larraza-Kintana, M. (2010). Socioemotional wealth and corporate responses to institutional pressures: Do family-controlled firms pollute less? *Administrative Science Quarterly*, 55, 82–113.

Besharov, M. (2014). The relational ecology of identification: How organizational identification emerges when individuals hold divergent values. *Academy of Management Journal*, 57, 1485–1512.

Besharov, M. L. & Brickson, S. L. (2016). Organizational identity and institutional forces: Toward an integrative framework. In M. G. Pratt, M. Schultz, B. E. Ashforth et al., eds., *The Oxford Handbook of Organizational Identity*. Oxford: Oxford University Press, 396-414.

Biggart, N. W. & Beamish, T. D. (2003). The economic sociology of conventions: Habit, custom, practice and routine in market order. *Annual Review of Sociology*, 29, 443-64.

Boghossian, J. (2017). Artisans of authenticity: The emergence and growth of markets for artisan cheese and wine in Quebec. *Strategy and Organization*. Montreal: McGill University, 1-189.

Boghossian, J. & David, R. (2017). Artisans of Authenticity: Identity Construction and Market Category Emergence.

Bono, J. E., Foldes, H. J., Vinson, G. & Muros, J. P. (2007). Workplace emotions: The role of supervision and leadership. *Journal of Applied Psychology*, 92(5), 1357.

Borgatti, S. & Halgin, D. (2011). On network theory. *Organization Science*, 22(5), 1168-81.

Bourdieu, P. (2000). *Pascalian Meditations*. Stanford, CA: Stanford University Press.

Brescoll, V. L. & Uhlmann, E. L. (2008). Can an angry woman get ahead? Status conferral, gender, and expression of emotion in the workplace. *Psychological Science*, 19(3), 268-75.

Breugst, N., Domurath, A., Patzelt, H. & Klaukien, A. (2012). Perceptions of entrepreneurial passion and employees' commitment to entrepreneurial ventures. *Entrepreneurship: Theory and Practice*, 36, 171-92.

Briscoe, F. & Safford, S. (2008). The Nixon-in China effect: Activism, imitation and the institutionalization of contentious practices. *Administrative Science Quarterly*, 53(3), 460-91.

Bröer, C. & Duyvendak, J. (2009). Discursive opportunities, feeling rules, and the rise of protests against aircraft noise. *Mobilization: An International Quarterly*, 14, 337-56.

Brown, A. D. (1997). Narcissism, identity, and legitimacy. *Academy of Management Review*, 22, 643-86.

Brown, A. D., Ainsworth, S. & Grant, D. (2012). The rhetoric of institutional change. *Organization Studies*, 33, 297-321.

Burt, R. S. (1992). *Structural Holes: The Social Structure of Competition*. Cambridge, MA: Harvard University Press.

Calhoun, C. (2001). Putting emotions in their place. In J. Goodwin, J. M. Jasper & F. Polletta, eds., *Passionate Politics: Emotions and Social Movements*. Chicago, IL: University of Chicago Press, 45-57.

Cardon, M. S., Post, C. & Forster, W. (2017). Team entrepreneurial passion (TEP): Its emergence and influence in new venture teams. *Academy of Management Review*, 42(2), 283–305.

Cardon, M. S., Wincent, J., Singh, J. & Drnovsek, M. (2009). The nature and experience of entrepreneurial passion. *Academy of Management Review*, 34(3), 511–32.

Cardon, M. S., Zietsma, C., Saparito, P., Matherne, B. & Davis, C. (2005). A tale of passion: New insights into entrepreneurship from a parenthood analogy. *Journal of Business Venturing*, 20(1), 23–45.

Carr, A. (1998). Identity, compliance and dissent in organizations: A psychoanalytic perspective. *Organization*, 5, 81–99.

Carr, A. (2001). Understanding emotion and emotionality in a process of change. *Journal of Organizational Change Management*, 14, 421–34.

Carroll, G. R. & Swaminathan, A. (1992). The organizational ecology of strategic groups in the American brewing industry from 1975 to 1990. *Industrial and Corporate Change*, 1, 65–97.

Carroll, G. R. & Swaminathan, A. (2000). Why the microbrewery movement? Organizational dynamics of resource partitioning in the US brewing industry. *American Journal of Sociology*, 106(3), 715–62.

Casciaro, T., Gino, F. & Kouchaki, M. (2014). The contaminating effects of building instrumental ties: How networking can make us feel dirty. *Administrative Science Quarterly*, 59(4), 705–35.

Casciaro, T. & Piskorski, M. J. (2005). Power imbalance, mutual dependence and constraint absorption: A closer look at resource dependence theory. *Administrative Science Quarterly*, 50(2), 167–99.

Cascón-Pereira, R. & Hallier, J. (2012). Getting that certain feeling: The role of emotions in the meaning, construction and enactment of doctor managers' identities. *British Journal of Management*, 23, 130–44.

Catino, M. & Patriotta, G. (2013). Learning from errors: Cognition, emotions and safety culture in the Italian air force. *Organization Studies*, 34(4), 437–67

Chen, X. P., Yao, X. & Kotha, S. (2009). Entrepreneur passion and prepared-ness in business plan presentations: A persuasion analysis of venture capitalists' funding decisions. *Academy of Management Journal*, 52(1), 199–214.

Clancy, A., Vince, R. & Gabriel, Y. (2012). That unwanted feeling: A psychodynamic study of disappointment in organizations. *British Journal of Management*, 23(4), 518–31.

Clegg, S. & Baumeler, C. (2010). Essai: From iron cages to liquid modernity in organization analysis. *Organization Studies*, 31(12), 1713–33.

Collewaert, V., Anseel, F., Crommelinck, M., De Beuckelaer, A. & Vermeire, J. (2016). When passion fades: Disentangling the temporal dynamics of entrepreneurial passion for founding. *Journal of Management Studies*, 53, 966–95.

Collins, R. (2004). *Interaction Ritual Chains*. Princeton, NJ: Princeton University Press.

Collins, R. (2001). Social movements and the focus of emotional attention. In J. Goodwin, J. M. Jasper & F. Polletta, eds., *Passionate Politics: Emotions and Social Movements*. Chicago, IL: University of Chicago Press, 27–44.

Conroy, S. A. & O'Leary-Kelly, A. M. (2014). Letting go and moving on: Work-related identity loss and recovery. *Academy of Management Review*, 39, 67–87.

Corley, K. G. & Gioia, D. A. (2004). Identity ambiguity and change in the wake of a corporate spin-off. *Administrative Science Quarterly*, 49, 173–208.

Cornelissen, J. P., Mantere, S. & Vaara, E. (2014). The contraction of meaning: The combined effect of communication, emotions, and materiality on sensemaking in the Stockwell shooting. *Journal of Management Studies*, 51, 699–736.

Coupland, C., Brown, A. D., Daniels, K., et al. (2008). Saying it with feeling: Analysing speakable emotions. *Human Relations*, 61, 327–53.

Courpasson, D. & Monties, V. (2017). "I am my body." Physical selves of police officers in a changing institution. *Journal of Management Studies*, 54, 32–57.

Coviello, N. (2006). The network dynamics of international new ventures. *Journal of International Business Studies*, 37(5), 713–31.

Craib, L. (1988). *Experiencing Identity*. London: Sage Publications.

Creed, D., Hudson, B., Okhuysen, G. & Smith-Crowe, K. (2014). Swimming in a sea of shame: Incorporating emotion into explanations of institutional reproduction and change. *Academy of Management Review*, 39, 275–301.

Creed, W. E. D., DeJordy, R. & Lok, J. (2010). Being the change: Resolving institutional contradiction through identity work. *Academy of Management Journal*, 53, 1336–64.

Creed, W. E. D., Hudson, B. A., Okhuysen, G. A., et al. (2014). Swimming in a sea of shame: Incorporating emotion into explanations of institutional reproduction and change. *Academy of Management Review*, 39, 275–301.

Crook, T. R., Combs, J. G., Ketchen, D. J. & Aguinis, H. (2013). Organizing around transaction costs: What have we learned and where do we go from here? *Academy of Management Perspectives*, 27(1), 63–79.

Crossan, M. M., Maurer, C. C. & White, R. E. (2011). Reflections on the 2009 AMR decade award: Do we have a theory of organizational learning? *Academy of Management Review*, 36(3), 446–60.

Curchod, C., Patriotta, G. & Neysen, N. (2014). Categorization and identification: The identity work of "business sellers" on eBay. *Human Relations*, 67, 1293–1320.

Dahlander, L. & McFarland, D. A. (2013). Ties that last: Tie formation and persistence in research collaborations over time. *Administrative Science Quarterly*, 58(1), 69–110.

Davis, G. F. & Cobb, J. A. (2010). Resource dependence theory: Past and future. *Research in the Sociology of Organizations*, 1–31.

de Rond, M. & Lok, J. (2016). Some things can never be unseen: The role of context in psychological injury at war. *Academy of Management Journal*, 59, 1965–93.

DeJordy, R. & Barrett, F. (2014). Emotions in institutions: Bullying as a mechanism of institutional control. *Research on Emotion in Organizations*, 10, 219–44.

Delmestri, G. & Goodrick, E. (2017). Looking away: Denial and emotions in institutional stability and change. In *How Institutions Matter! Research in the Sociology of Organizations*, vol. 48A. Bingley, UK: Emerald Publishing, 233–71.

Delmestri, G. & Greenwood, R. (2016). How Cinderella became a queen: Theorizing radical status change. *Administrative Science Quarterly*, 61(4), 507–50.

DiMaggio, P. & Powell, W. W. (1983). The iron cage revisited: Collective rationality and institutional isomorphism in organizational fields. *American Sociological Review*, 48(2), 147–60.

Doern, R. & Goss, D. (2014). The role of negative emotions in the social processes of entrepreneurship: Power rituals and shame-related appeasement behaviors. *Entrepreneurship Theory and Practice*, 38(4), 863–90.

Dong, Y., Seo, M. G. & Bartol, K. M. (2014). No pain, no gain: An affect-based model of developmental job experience and the buffering effects of emotional intelligence. *Academy of Management Journal*, 57(4), 1056–77.

Driver, M. (2009). Struggling with lack: A Lacanian perspective on organizational identity. *Organization Studies*, 30, 55–72.

Dukerich, J. M., Golden, B. R. & Shortell, S. M. (2002). Beauty is in the eye of the beholder: The impact of organizational identification, identity, and image on the cooperative behaviors of physicians. *Administrative Science Quarterly*, 47, 507–33.

Durkheim, E. (1915). The elementary forms of the religious life, trans. Joseph Ward Swain (New York, 1915). In Edward Shils, ed., *Center and Periphery: Essays in Macrosociology* (Chicago, IL, 1975).

Dutton, J. E. & Dukerich, J. M. (1991). Keeping an eye on the mirror: Image, and identity in organizational adaptation. *Academy of Management Journal*, 34, 517 54.

Dutton, J. E., Roberts, L. M. & Bednar, J. (2011). Using a positive lens to complicate the positive in identity research. *Academy of Management Review*, 36, 427–31.

Ebaugh, H. R. F. (1988). *Becoming an Ex: The Process of Role Exit*. Chicago, IL: University of Chicago Press.

Elfenbein, H. A. (2007). Emotion in organizations: A review and theoretical integration. *Academy of Management Annals*, 1(1), 315–86.

Elias, S. R. S. T. A., Chiles, T. H., Duncan, C. M. & Vultee, D. M. (2018). The aesthetics of entrepreneurship: How arts entrepreneurs and their customers co-create aesthetic value. *Organization Studies*, 39(2–3), 345–72.

Elsbach, K. D. & Kramer, R. M. (1996). Members' responses to organizational identity threats: Encountering and countering the business week rankings. *Administrative Science Quarterly*, 41, 442–76.

Emirbayer, M. (1997). Manifesto for a relational sociology. *American Journal of Sociology*, 103(2), 281–317.

Emirbayer, M. & Goldberg, C. A. (2005). Pragmatism, Bourdieu, and collective emotions in contentious politics. *Theory and Society*, 34, 469–518.

Endrissat, N., Islam, G. & Noppeney, C. (2015). Enchanting work: New spirits of service work in an organic supermarket. *Organization Studies*, 36(11), 1555–76.

Fama, E. F. & Jensen, M. C. (1983). Agency problems and residual claims. *Journal of Law and Economics*, 36, 327–49.

Fan, G. H. & Zietsma, C. (2017). Constructing a shared governance logic: The role of emotions in enabling dually embedded agency. *Academy of Management Journal*, 60(6), 2321–51.

Farney, S., Kibler, E. & Down, S. (forthcoming). Collective emotions in institutional creation work. *Academy of Management Journal*.

Fauchart, E. & Gruber, M. (2011). Darwinians, communitarians, and missionaries: The role of founder identity in entrepreneurship. *Academy of Management Journal*, 54(5), 935–57.

Fehr, R., Fulmer, A., Awtrey, E. & Miller, J. A. (2017). The grateful workplace: A multilevel model of gratitude in organizations. *Academy of Management Review*, 42(2), 361–81.

Fineman, S. (2000). *Emotion in Organizations*. Newbury Park, CA: Sage Publications.

Fineman, S. (2003). *Understanding Emotion at Work*. London: Sage Publications.

Fineman, S. (2004). Getting the measure of emotion – and the cautionary tale of emotional intelligence. *Human Relations*, 57, 719–40.

Fineman, S. (2006). Emotion and organizing. In S. Clegg, C. Hardy, T. B. Lawrence & W. R. Nord, eds., *The Sage Handbook of Organization Studies*. London: Sage Publications, 675–700.

Fineman, S. (2006). On being positive: Concerns and counterpoints. *Academy of Management Review*, 31, 270–91.

Fineman, S. (2008). Getting the measure of emotion: And the cautionary tale of emotional intelligence. *Emotions: A Social Science Reader*. London and New York, NY: Routledge.

Fineman, S. & Sturdy, A. (1999). The emotions of control: A qualitative exploration of environmental regulation. *Human Relations*, 52(5), 631–63.

Fiol, C. M. (2002). Capitalizing on paradox: The role of language in transforming organizational identities. *Organization Science*, 13, 653–66.

Fleming, P. (2009). *Authenticity and the Cultural Politics of Work: New Forms of Informal Control*. Oxford: Oxford University Press.

Fleming, P. & Spicer, A. (2007). *Contesting the Corporation: Struggle, Power and Resistance*. Cambridge: Cambridge University Press.

Fleming, P. & Spicer, A. (2014). Power in management and organization science. *Academy of Management Annals*, 8(1), 237–98.

Fligstein, N. & Dauter, L. (2007). The sociology of markets. *Annual Review of Sociology*, 33, 105–28.

Follett, M. P. (1927). *Dynamic Administration* (reprint 1942). New York, NY: Harper & Brothers Publishers.

Foo, M. D., Sin, H. P. & Yiong, L. P. (2006). Effects of team inputs and intrateam processes on perceptions of team viability and member satisfaction in nascent ventures. *Strategic Management Journal*, 27(4), 389–99.

Ford, J. D., Ford, L. W. & McNamara, R. T. (2002) Resistance and the background conversations of change. *Journal of Organizational Change Management*, 15(2), 105–21.

Foreman, P. & Whetten, D. A. (2002). Members' identification with multiple-identity organizations. *Organization Science*, 13, 618–35.

Fotaki, M., Kenny, K. & Vachhani, S. J. (2017). Thinking critically about affect in organization studies: Why it matters. *Organization*, 24(1), 3–17.

Foucault, M. (1977). *Discipline & Punish*. Toronto: Random House.

Fraher, A. L. & Gabriel, Y. (2014). Dreaming of flying when grounded: Occupational identity and occupational fantasies of furloughed airline pilots. *Journal of Management Studies*, 51, 926–51.

Friedland, R. (2013). Review: The institutional logics perspective: A new approach to culture, structure, and process. *M@n@gement*, 15, 583–95.

Friedland, R. (2018). Moving institutional logics forward: Emotion and meaningful material practice. *Organization Studies*, 39(4), 515–42.

Friedland, R., Mohr, J., Roose, H. & Gardinali, P. (2014) The institutional logics of love: Measuring intimate life. *Theory and Society*, 43(3–4), 333–70.

Frijda, N. H. (1988). The laws of emotion. *American Psychologist*, 43(5), 349.

Frost, P. J., Dutton, J. E., Worline, M. C. & Wilson, A. (2000). Narratives of compassion in organizations. *Emotion in Organizations*, 2, 25–45.

Gabriel, Y. & Griffiths, D. S. (2002). Emotion, learning and organizing. *Learning Organization*, 9(5), 214–21.

Gambetta, D. (1988). Can we trust trust? In D. Gambetta, ed., *Trust: Making and Breaking Cooperative Relations*.

Gehman, J., Trevino, L. K. & Garud, R. (2013). Values work: A process study of the emergence and performance of organizational values practices. *Academy of Management Journal*, 56, 84–112.

Gendron, Y. & Spira, L. F. (2010). Identity narratives under threat: A study of former members of Arthur Andersen. *Accounting, Organizations and Society*, 35, 275–300.

Ghoshal, S. (2005). Bad management theories are destroying good management practices. *Academy of Management Learning & Education*, 4(1), 75–91.

Gielnik, M. M., Spitzmuller, M., Schmitt, A., Klemann, D. K. & Frese, M. (2015). "I put in effort, therefore I am passionate": Investigating the path from effort to passion in entrepreneurship. *Academy of Management Journal*, 58(4), 1012–31.

Gill, M. J. & Burrow, R. (2018). The function of fear in institutional maintenance: Feeling frightened as an essential ingredient in haute cuisine. *Organization Studies*, 39(4), 445–66.

Gioia, D. A. & Chittipeddi, K. (1991). Sensemaking and sensegiving in strategic change initiation. *Strategic Management Journal*, 12, 433–48.

Gioia, D. A. & Thomas, J. B. (1996). Identity, image, and issue interpretation: Sensemaking during strategic change in academia. *Administrative Science Quarterly*, 41, 370–403.

Gioia, D. A., Patvardhan, S. D, Hamilton, A. L, et al. (2013). Organizational identity formation and change. *Academy of Management Annals*, 7, 123–93.

Giorgi, S. (2017). The mind and heart of resonance: The role of cognition and emotions in frame effectiveness. *Journal of Management Studies*, 54, 711–38.

Giorgi, S., Guider, M. E. & Bartunek, J. M. (2014). Productive resistance: A study of change, emotions, and identity in the context of the apostolic visitation of U.S. women religious, 2008–2012. *Research in the Sociology of Organizations*, 41, 259–300.

Giorgi, S. & Palmisano, S. (2017). Sober intoxication: Institutional contradictions and identity work in the everyday life of four religious communities in Italy. *Organization Studies*, 38(6), 795–819.

Glynn, M. A. (2008). Beyond constraint: How institutions enable identities. In R. Greenwood, C. Oliver, K. Sahlin, et al., eds., *The Sage Handbook of Organizational Institutionalism*, London: Sage Publications, 413–30.

Glynn, M. A. (2017). Theorizing the identity–institution relationship: Considering identity as antecedent to, consequences of, and mechanisms for, processes of institutional change. In R. Greenwood, C. Oliver, T. B. Lawrence, et al., eds., *The Sage Handbook of Organizational Institutionalism*. 2nd edn. London: Sage Publications.

Glynn, M. A. & Navis, C. (2013). Categories, identities, and cultural classification: Moving beyond a model of categorical constraint. *Journal of Management Studies*, 50(6), 1124–37.

Goffman, E. (1959). *The Presentation of Self in Everyday Life*. Garden City, NY: Doubleday.

Gómez-Mejía, L. R., Haynes, K. T., Núñez-Nickel, M., Jacobson, K. L. & Moyano-Fuentes, J. (2007). Socioemotional wealth and business risks in family-controlled firms: Evidence from Spanish olive oil mills. *Administrative Science Quarterly*, 52(1), 106–37.

Goodwin, J. (1997). The libidinal constitution of a high-risk social movement: Affectual ties and solidarity in the Huk rebellion, 1946 to 1954. *American Sociological Review*, 62, 53–69.

Goodwin, J. & Jasper, J. M. (2006). Emotions and social movements. In J. E. Stets and J. H. Turner, eds., *Handbook of the Sociology of Emotions*. New York, NY: Springer, 611–36.

Goodwin, J., Jasper, J., & Polletta, F. (2001). *Passionate Politics: Emotions and Social Movements*. Chicago, IL: University of Chicago Press.

Goodwin, J. & Pfaff, S. (2001). Emotion work in high-risk social movements. In J. Goodwin, J. M. Jasper & F. Polletta, eds., *Passionate Politics: Emotions and Social Movements*. Chicago, IL: University of Chicago Press, 282–302.

Gooty, J., Gavin, M. & Ashkanasy, N. M. (2009). Emotions research in OB: The challenges that lie ahead. *Journal of Organizational Behavior*, 30(6), 833–38.

Goss, D. (2008). Enterprise ritual: A theory of entrepreneurial emotion and exchange. *British Journal of Management*, 19(2), 120–37.

Gould, D. (2009). *Moving Politics: Emotion and ACT UP's Fight against AIDS*. Chicago, IL: University of Chicago Press.

Gouldner, A. (1954). *Patterns of Industrial Bureaucracy*. Glencoe, IL: Free Press.

Grandey, A. A. (2008). Emotions at work: A review and research agenda. *Handbook of Organizational Behavior*, 235–61.

Granovetter, M. (1985). Economic action and social structure: The problem of embeddedness. *American Journal of Sociology*, 91, 481–510.

Granovetter, M. S. (1973). The strength of weak ties. *American Journal of Sociology*, 78(6), 1360–80.

Grant, A. M. (2013). Rocking the boat but keeping it steady: The role of emotion regulation in employee voice. *Academy of Management Journal*, 56(6), 1703–23.

Grodal, S. & Granqvist, N. (2014). Great expectations: Discourse and affect during field emergence. *Research on Emotion in Organizations*, 10, 139–66.

Grodal, S., Nelson, A. J. & Siino, R. M. (2015). Help-seeking and help-giving as an organizational routine: Continual engagement in innovative work. *Academy of Management Journal*, 58, 136–68.

Gulati, R. (1995). Social structure and alliance formation patterns: A longitudinal analysis. *Administrative Science Quarterly*, 40(4), 619–52.

Gulati, R. & Sytch, M. (2007). Dependence asymmetry and joint dependence in interorganizational relationships: Effects of embeddedness on a manufacturer's performance in procurement relationships. *Administrative Science Quarterly*, 52(1), 32–69.

Gutierrez, B., Howard-Grenville, J. & Scully, M. A. (2010). The faithful rise up: Split identification and an unlikely change effort. *Academy of Management Journal*, 53, 673–99.

Haack, P., Pfarrer, M. D. & Scherer, A. G. (2014). Legitimacy-as-feeling: How affect leads to vertical legitimacy spillovers in transnational governance. *Journal of Management Studies*, 51, 634–66.

Haack, P. & Sieweke, J. (2018). The legitimacy of inequality: Integrating the perspectives of system justification and social judgment. *Journal of Management Studies*, 55(3), 486–516.

Haidt, J. (2012). *The Righteous Mind: Why Good People Are Divided by Politics and Religion*. New York, NY: Vintage.

Hallett, T. (2003). Symbolic power and organizational culture. *Sociological Theory*, 21(2), 128–49.

Hallett, T. (2010). The myth incarnate: Recoupling processes, turmoil, and inhabited institutions in an urban elementary school. *American Sociological Review*, 75, 52–74.

Hallett, T. & Ventresca, M. J. (2006). Inhabited institutions: Social interactions and organizational forms in Gouldner's "patterns of industrial bureaucracy." *Theory and Society*, 35, 213–36.

Hamilton, L. & McCabe, D. (2016). "It's just a job": Understanding emotion work, de-animalization and the compartmentalization of organized animal slaughter. *Organization*, 23(3), 330–50.

Hancock, P. & Tyler, M. (2001). *Work, Postmodernism and Organization: A Critical Introduction*. Sage Publications.

Hannan, M. T., Pólos, L. & Carroll, G. R. (2007). *Logics of Organization Theory: Audiences, Codes, and Ecologies*. Princeton, NJ: Princeton University Press.

Hardy, C. & Clegg, S. (2006). Some dare call it power. In S. Clegg, C. Hardy, T. B. Lawrence & W. R. Nord, eds., *The Sage Handbook of Organization Studies*. London: Sage Publications, 754–75.

Hareli, S. & Rafaeli, A. (2008). Emotion cycles: On the social influence of emotion in organizations. *Research in Organizational Behavior*, 28, 35–59.

Harmon, D. J., Green, S. E. & Goodnight, G. T. (2015). A model of rhetorical legitimation: The structure of communication and cognition underlying institutional maintenance and change. *Academy of Management Review*, 40, 76–95.

Harmon, D. (forthcoming). When the fed speaks: Arguments, emotions, and the micro-foundations of Institutions. *Administrative Science Quarterly*.

Harquail, C. V. & Wilcox King, A. (2010). Construing organizational identity: The role of embodied cognition. *Organization Studies*, 31, 1619–48.

Hatch, M. J. (1993). The dynamics of organizational culture. *Academy of Management Review*, 18(4), 657–93.

Hatch, M. J. & Schultz, M. (2017). Toward a theory of using history authentically: Historicizing in the Carlsberg Group. *Administrative Science Quarterly*, 62(4), 657–97.

Hatch, M. J., Schultz, M. & Skov, A. M. (2015). Organizational identity and culture in the context of managed change: Transformation in the Carlsberg group, 2009–2013. *Academy of Management Discoveries*, 1, 58–90.

Hatch, M. J. & Zilber, T. (2012). Conversation at the border between organizational culture theory and institutional theory. *Journal of Management Inquiry*, 21(1), 94–97.

He, H. & Brown, A. D. (2013). Organizational identity and organizational identification: A review of the literature and suggestions for future research. *Group and Organization Management*, 38, 3–35.

Heaphy, E. D. (2017) "Dancing on hot coals": How emotion work facilitates collective sensemaking. *Academy of Management Journal*, 60, 642–70.

Herscovitch, L. & Meyer, J. P. (2002). Commitment to organizational change: Extension of a three-component model. *Journal of Applied Psychology*, 87(3), 474.

Hiatt, S. R. & Sine, W. D. (2014). Clear and present danger: Planning and new venture survival amid political and civil violence. *Strategic Management Journal*, 35(5), 773–785.

Hiatt, S. R., Sine, W. D. & Tolbert, P. S. (2009). From Pabst to Pepsi: The deinstitutionalization of social practices and the creation of entrepreneurial opportunities. *Administrative Science Quarterly*, 54(4), 635–67.

Hillman, A. J., Withers, M. C. & Collins, B. J. (2009) Resource dependence theory: A review. *Journal of Management*, 35(6), 1404–27.

Hite, J. & Hesterly, W. (2001). The evolution of firm networks: From emergence to early growth of the firm. *Strategic Management Journal*, 22(3), 275–86.

Hochschild, A. R. (1979). Emotion work, feeling rules and social structure. *American Journal of Sociology*, 85, 551–75.

Hochschild, A. R. (1983). *The Managed Heart: Commercialization of Human Feeling*. Berkeley, CA: University of California Press.

Hochschild, A. R. (2016). *Strangers in Their Own Land: Anger and Mourning on the American Right*. New York, NY: New Press.

Hochschild, A. & Machung, A. (2012). *The Second Shift: Working Families and the Revolution at Home*. New York, NY: Penguin.

Howard-Grenville, J., Metzger, M. L. & Meyer, A. D. (2013). Rekindling the flame: Processes of identity resurrection. *Academy of Management Journal*, 56, 113–36.

Hsu, G., Koçak, Ö. & Hannan, M. T. (2009). Multiple category memberships in markets: An integrative theory and two empirical tests. *American Sociological Review*, 74, 150–69.

Huang, L. & Knight, A. P. (2017). Resources and relationships in entrepreneurship: An exchange theory of the development and effects of the entrepreneur-investor relationship. *Academy of Management Review*, 42 (1), 80–102.

Hudson, B., Okhuysen, G. & Creed, W. (2015). Power and institutions: Stones in the road and some yellow bricks. *Journal of Management Inquiry*, 24, 233–38.

Humphrey, R. H., Ashforth, B. E. & Diefendorff, J. M. (2015). *The Bright Side of Emotional Labor*. New York, NY: John Wiley & Sons, Inc., 749–69.

Huy, Q. N. (1999). Emotional capability, emotional intelligence, and radical change. *Academy of Management Review*, 24(2), 325–45.

Huy, Q. N. (2002). Emotional balancing of organizational continuity and radical change: The contribution of middle managers. *Administrative Science Quarterly*, 47(1), 31–70.

Huy, Q. N. (2011). How middle managers' group-focus emotions and social identities influence strategy implementation. *Strategic Management Journal*, 32, 1387–1410.

Huy, Q. N., Corley, K. G. & Kraatz, M. S. (2014). From support to mutiny: Shifting legitimacy judgments and emotional reactions impacting the implementation of radical change. *Academy of Management Journal*, 57(6), 1650–80.

Ibarra, H. (1999). Provisional selves: Experimenting with image and identity in professional adaptation. *Administrative Science Quarterly*, 44, 764–91.

Ibarra, H. & Barbulescu, R. (2010). Identity as narrative: Prevalence, effectiveness, and consequences of narrative identity work in macro role transitions. *Academy of Management Review*, 35, 135–54.

Illouz, E. (2007). *Cold Intimacies: The Making of Emotional Capitalism*. Cambridge: Polity.

Illouz, E., Gilon, D. & Shachak, M. (2014). Emotions and cultural theory. In *Handbook of the Sociology of Emotions*. Vol. II. Dordrecht: Springer, 221–44.

Jakob-Sadeh, L. & Zilber, T. B. (forthcoming). Bringing "together": Emotions and power in organizational responses to institutional complexity. *Academy of Management Journal*.

Jarvis, L. C. (2017). Feigned versus felt: Feigning behaviors and the dynamics of institutional logics. *Academy of Management Review*, 42, 306–33.

Jarvis, L. C., Goodrick, E. & Hudson, B. A. (forthcoming). Where the heart functions best: Reactive-affective conflict and the disruptive work of animal rights organizations. *Academy of Management Journal*.

Jarzabkowski, P. A. & Lê, J. K. (2017). We have to do this and that? You must be joking: Constructing and responding to paradox through humor. *Organization Studies*, 38, 433–62.

Jasper, J. M. (2006). *Getting Your Way: Strategic Dilemmas in the Real World*. Chicago, IL: University of Chicago Press.

Jasper, J. M. (2011). Emotions and social movements: Twenty years of theory and research. *Annual Review of Sociology*, 37, 285–303.

Jasper, J. M. & Poulsen, J. D. (1995). Recruiting strangers and friends: Moral shocks and social networks in animal rights and antinuclear protests. *Social Problems*, 42, 493–512.

Jennings, J. E., Edwards, T., Jennings, P. D. & Delbridge, R. (2015). Emotional arousal and entrepreneurial outcomes: Combining qualitative methods to elaborate theory. *Journal of Business Venturing*, 30(1), 113–30.

Jensen, M. C. & Meckling, W. H. (1976). Theory of the firm: Managerial behavior, agency costs and ownership structure. *Journal of Financial Economics*, 3(4), 305–60.

Joseph, D. L. & Newman, D. A. (2010). Emotional intelligence: An integrative meta-analysis and cascading model. *Journal of Applied Psychology*, 95(1), 54.

Kaplan, S. (2008). Framing contests: Strategy making under uncertainty. *Organization Science*, 19, 729–52.

Kelly, J. R. & Barsade, S. G. (2001). Mood and emotions in small groups and work teams. *Organizational Behavior and Human Decision Processes*, 86(1), 99–130.

Keltner, D. & Haidt, J. (1999). Social functions of emotions at four levels of analysis. *Cognition & Emotion*, 13(5), 505–21.

Kennedy, H. & Hill, R. L. (2017). The feeling of numbers: Emotions in everyday engagements with data and their visualization. *Sociology*.

Kenny, K. (2012). "Someone big and important": Identification and affect in an international development organization. *Organization Studies*, 33(9), 1175–93.

Khaire, M. & Wadhwani, R. D. (2010). Changing landscapes: The construction of meaning and value in a new market category – modern Indian art. *Academy of Management Journal*, 53(6), 1281–1304.

King, B. G. & Pearce, N. (2010). The contentiousness of markets: Politics, social movements, and institutional change in markets. *Annual Review of Sociology*, 36, 249–67.

Kjærgaard, A., Morsing, M. & Ravasi, D. (2011). Mediating identity: A study of media influence on organizational identity construction in a celebrity firm. *Journal of Management Studies*, 48, 514–43.

Koçak, Ö., Hannan, M. T. & Hsu, G. (2014). Emergence of market orders: Audience interaction and vanguard influence. *Organization Studies*, 35(5), 765–90.

Koerner, M. M. (2014). Courage as identity work: Accounts of workplace courage. *Academy of Management Journal*, 57, 63–93.

Kraatz, M. S. & Block, E. (2008). Organizational implications of institutional pluralism. In R. Greenwood, C. Oliver, R. Suddaby, et al., eds. *Handbook of Organizational Institutionalism*. Thousand Oaks, CA: Sage Publications, 243–75.

Kunda, G. (1995). Engineering culture: Control and commitment in a high-tech corporation. *Organization Science*, 6(2), 228–30.

Larson, A. (1992). Network dyads in entrepreneurial settings: A study of the governance of exchange relationships. *Administrative Science Quarterly*, 37(1), 76–104.

Lawrence T. B. (in press). High stakes institutional translation: Establishing North America's first government-sanctioned supervised injection site. *Academy of Management Journal*.

Lawrence, T. B., Leca, B. & Zilber, T. B. (2013). Institutional work: Current research, new directions and overlooked issues. *Organization Studies*, 34, 1023–33.

Lawrence, T. B. & Maitlis, S. (2012). Care and possibility: Enacting an ethic of care through narrative practice. *Academy of Management Review*, 37(4), 641–63.

Lawrence, T. B. & Phillips, N. (2004). From Moby Dick to Free Willy: Macro-cultural discourse and institutional entrepreneurship in emerging institutional fields. *Organization*, 11(5), 689–711.

Lee, B. H., Hiatt, S. R. & Lounsbury, M. (2017). Market mediators and the trade-offs of legitimacy-seeking behaviors in a nascent category. *Organization Science*.

Leung, A., Zietsma, C. & Peredo, A. M. (2014). Emergent identity work and institutional change: The "quiet" revolution of Japanese middle-class housewives. *Organization Studies*, 35, 423–50.

Lichtenstein, G. A. & Lyons, T. S. (2010). *Investing in Entrepreneurs: A Strategic Approach for Strengthening Your Regional and Community Economy*. Santa Barbara, CA: Praeger/ABC-CLIO.

Lilius, J. M., Worline, M. C., Dutton, J. E., Kanov, J. M. & Maitlis, S. (2011). Understanding compassion capability. *Human Relations*, 64(7), 873–99.

Lindebaum, D. (2017). *Emancipation through Emotional Regulation at Work*. Cheltenham, UK: Edward Elgar Publishing.

Lindebaum, D. & Gabriel, Y. (2016). Anger and organization studies: From social disorder to moral order. *Organization Studies*, 37(7), 903–18.

Liu, F. & Maitlis, S. (2014). Emotional dynamics and strategizing processes: A study of strategic conversations in top team meetings. *Journal of Management Studies*, 51(2), 202–34.

Llewellyn, N. & Spence, L. (2009). Practice as a members' phenomenon. *Organization Studies*, 30, 1419–39.

Lok, J. (2010). Institutional logics as identity projects. *Academy of Management Journal*, 53, 1305–35.

Lok, J., Creed, W. E. D., DeJordy R., et al. (2017). Living institutions: Bringing emotions into organizational institutionalism. In R. Greenwood, C. Oliver, T. B. Lawrence, et al., eds., *The Sage Handbook of Organizational Institutionalism*. 2nd edn. London: Sage Publications, 591–620.

Lok, J. & De Rond, M. (2013). On the plasticity of institutions: Containing and restoring practice breakdowns at the Cambridge University boat club. *Academy of Management Journal*, 56, 185–207.

Lord, R. G., Dinh, J. E. & Hoffman, E. L. (2015). A quantum approach to time and organizational change. *Academy of Management Review*, 40(2), 263–90.

Lounsbury, M. & Glynn, M. A. (2001). Cultural entrepreneurship: Stories, legitimacy, and the acquisition of resources. *Strategic Management Journal*, 22( 6–7), 545–64.

Lounsbury, M., Ventresca, M. & Hirsch, P. M. (2003). Social movements, field frames and industry emergence: A cultural-political perspective on US recycling. *Socio-Economic Review*, 1, 71–104.

Mair, J., Martí, I., & Ventresca, M. (2012). Building inclusive markets in rural Bangladesh: How intermediaries work institutional voids. *Academy of Management Journal*, 55(4), 819–50.

Maitlis, S. (2005). The social processes of organizational sensemaking. *Academy of Management Journal*, 48(1), 21–49.

Maitlis, S. & Christianson, M. (2014). Sensemaking in organizations: Taking stock and moving forward. *Academy of Management Annals*, 8, 57–125.

Maitlis, S. & Lawrence, T. B. (2007). Triggers and enablers of sensegiving in organizations. *Academy of Management Journal*, 50, 57–84.

Maitlis, S. & Sonenshein, S. (2010) Sensemaking in crisis and change: Inspiration and insights from Weick (1988). *Journal of Management Studies*, 47, 551–80.

Maitlis, S., Vogus, T. J. & Lawrence, T. B. (2013). Sensemaking and emotion in organizations. *Organizational Psychology Review*, 3, 222–47.

March, J. G. & Simon, H. A. (1958). *Organizations*. New York, NY: Wiley.

Marquis, C. & Lounsbury, M. (2007). Vive la résistance: Competing logics and the consolidation of US Community banking. *Academy of Management Journal*, 50, 799–820.

Martí, I., Courpasson, D. & Barbosa, S. D. (2013). "Living in the fishbowl": Generating an entrepreneurial culture in a local community in Argentina. *Journal of Business Venturing*, 28(1), 10–29.

Martin, A. J., Jones, E. S. & Callan, V. J. (2005). The role of psychological climate in facilitating employee adjustment during organizational change. *European Journal of Work and Organizational Psychology*, 14(3), 263–89.

Martin, J., Knopoff, K. & Beckman, C. (1998). An alternative to bureaucratic impersonality and emotional labor: Bounded emotionality at the body shop. *Administrative Science Quarterly*, 43(2), 429–69.

Martin, P. Y. (2003). "Said and done" versus "saying and doing" gendering practices, practicing gender at work. *Gender and Society*, 17, 342–66.

Martin de Holan, P., Willi, A. & Fernández, P. D. (forthcoming). Breaking the wall: Emotions and projective agency under extreme poverty. *Business & Society.*

Massa, F. G. (2017). Guardians of the Internet: Building and sustaining the anonymous online community. *Organization Studies*, 38, 959–88.

Massa, F. G., Helms, W. S., Voronov, M. & Wang, L. (2017). Emotions uncorked: Inspiring evangelism for the emerging practice of cool-climate winemaking in Ontario. *Academy of Management Journal*, 60(2), 461–99.

Matthews, G., Zeidner, M. & Roberts, R. D. (2002). *Emotional Intelligence: Science and Myth.* Cambridge, MA: MIT Press.

Mayer, J. D. & Salovey, P. (1997). What is emotional intelligence? In P. Salovey & D. Sluyter, eds., *Emotional Development and Emotional Intelligence: Educational Implications.* New York, NY: Basic Books, 3–31.

McDermott, G. A., Corredoira, R. A. & Kruse, G. (2009). Public-private institutions as catalysts of upgrading in emerging market societies. *Academy of Management Journal*, 52(6), 1270–96.

McGonigal, J. (2011). *Reality Is Broken: Why Games Make Us Better and How They Can Change the World.* New York, NY: Penguin.

McKague, K., Zietsma, C. & Oliver, C. (2015). Building the social structure of a market. *Organization Studies*, 36(8), 1063–93.

McMurray, R. & Ward, J. (2014). "Why would you want to do that?" Defining emotional dirty work. *Human Relations*, 67, 1123–43.

Menges, J. I. & Kilduff, M. (2015). Group emotions: Cutting the Gordian knots concerning terms, levels of analysis, and processes. *Academy of Management Annals*, 9(1), 845–928.

Meyer, J. P., Srinivas, E. S., Lal, J. B. & Topolnytsky, L. (2007). Employee commitment and support for an organizational change: Test of the three-component model in two cultures. *Journal of Occupational and Organizational Psychology*, 80(2), 185–211.

Meyer, J. W. & Rowan, B. (1977). Institutionalized organizations: Formal structure as myth and ceremony. *American Journal of Sociology*, 83(2), 340–63.

Michel, A. (2011). Transcending socialization: A nine-year ethnography of the body's role in organizational control and knowledge workers' transformation. *Administrative Science Quarterly*, 56, 325–68.

Michel, A. (2014). The mutual constitution of persons and organizations: An ontological perspective on organizational change. *Organization Science*, 25(4), 1082–1110.

Miettinen, R., Samra-Fredericks, D. & Yanow, D. (2009). Return to practice: An introductory essay. *Organization Studies*, 30, 1309–27.

Miller, T. L., Grimes, M. G., McMullen, J. S. & Vogus, T. J. (2012). Venturing for others with heart and head: How compassion encourages social entrepreneurship. *Academy of Management Review*, 37(4), 616–40.

Mische, A. (2011). Relational sociology, culture, and agency. In J. Scott & P. J. Carrington, eds., *The Sage Handbook of Social Network Analysis*. London: Sage Publications, 80–97.

Mische, A. (2014). Measuring futures in action: Projective grammars in the Rio+ 20 debates. *Theory and Society*, 43(3–4), 437–64.

Mische, A. (2014). Relational sociology, culture and agency. In J. Scott and P. J. Carrington, eds., *The Sage Handbook of Social Network Analysis*. London: Sage Publications, 80–98.

Mitteness, C., Sudek, R. & Cardon, M. S. (2012). Angel investor characteristics that determine whether perceived passion leads to higher evaluations of funding potential. *Journal of Business Venturing*, 27(5), 592–606.

Moisander, J. K., Hirsto, H. & Fahy, K. M. (2016). Emotions in institutional work: A discursive perspective. *Organization Studies*, 37, 963–90.

Monaghan, S., Lavelle, J. & Gunnigle, P. (2017). Mapping networks: Exploring the utility of social network analysis in management research and practice. *Journal of Business Research*, 76, 136–44.

Montanari, F., Scapolan, A. & Gianecchini, M. (2016). "Absolutely free"? The role of relational work in sustaining artistic innovation. *Organization Studies*, 37(6), 797–821.

Moufahim, M., Reedy, P. & Humphreys, M. (2015). The vlaams belang: The rhetoric of organizational identity. *Organization Studies*, 36, 91–111.

Mumby, D. K. & Putnam, L. L. (1992). The politics of emotion: A feminist reading of bounded rationality. *Academy of Management Review*, 17(3), 465–86.

Murnieks, C. Y., McMullen, J. S. & Cardon, M. S. (2017). Does congruence with an entrepreneur social identity encourage positive emotion under environmental dynamism? *Journal of Small Business Management*.

Navis, C. & Glynn, M. A. (2010). How new market categories emerge: Temporal dynamics of legitimacy, identity, and entrepreneurship in satellite radio, 1990–2005. *Administrative Science Quarterly*, 55(3), 439–71.

Nicolini, D. (2009). Zooming in and out: Studying practices by switching theoretical lenses and trailing connections. *Organization Studies*, 30, 1391–1418.

Nicolini, D. (2012). *Practice Theory, Work and Organization: An Introduction*. Oxford: Oxford University Press.

Obodaru, O. (2012). The self not taken: How alternative selves develop and how they influence our professional lives. *Academy of Management Review*, 37, 34–57.

Obodaru, O. (2017). Forgone, but not forgotten: Toward a theory of forgone professional identities. *Academy of Management Journal* 60, 523–53.

Ody-Brasier, A. & Vermeulen, F. (2014). The price you pay: Price-setting as a response to norm violations in the market for champagne grapes. *Administrative Science Quarterly*, 59(1), 109–44.

O'Neill, O. A. & Rothbard, N. P. (2017). Is love all you need? The effects of emotional culture, suppression, and work–family conflict on firefighter risk-taking and health. *Academy of Management Journal*, 60(1), 78–108.

Oreg, S., Bartunek, J., Lee, G. & Do, B. (2018). An affect-based model of recipients' responses to organizational change events. *Academy of Management Review*, 43(1), 65–86.

Oreg, S., Vakola, M. & Armenakis, A. A. (2011). Change recipients' reactions to organizational change: A sixty-year review of quantitative studies. *Journal of Applied Behavioral Science*, 47(4), 461–524.

Paolella, L. & Durand, R. (2016). Category spanning, evaluation, and performance: Revised theory and test on the corporate law market. *Academy of Management Journal*, 59, 330–51.

Parke, M. R. & Seo, M. G. (2017). The role of affect climate in organizational effectiveness. *Academy of Management Review*, 42(2), 334–60.

Peli, G. (2009). Fit by founding, fit by adaptation: Reconciling conflicting organizational theories with logical formalization. *Academy of Management Review*, 34(2), 343–60.

Perugorria, I. & Tejerina, B. (2013). Politics of the encounter: Cognition, emotions and networks in the Spanish 15M. *Current Sociology*, 61(4), 424–42.

Petriglieri, G., Ashford, S. J. & Wrzesniewski, A. (forthcoming). Agony and ecstasy in the gig economy: Cultivating holding environments for precarious and personalized work identities. *Administrative Science Quarterly*.

Petriglieri, G. & Petriglieri, J. L. (2010). Identity workspaces: The case of business schools. *Academy of Management Learning and Education*, 9, 44–60.

Petriglieri, G., Petriglieri, J. L. & Wood, J. D. (forthcoming). Fast tracks and inner journeys: Crafting portable selves for contemporary careers. *Administrative Science Quarterly*.

Petriglieri, J. L. (2011). Under threat: Responses to the consequences of threats to individuals' identities. *Academy of Management Review*, 36, 641–62.

Petriglieri, J. L. (2015). Co-creating relationship repair: Pathways to reconstructing destabilized organizational identification. *Administrative Science Quarterly*, 60, 518–57.

Pfeffer, J. & Salancik, G. R. (1978). *The External Control of Organizations: A Resource Dependence Perspective.* New York, NY: Harper and Row Publishers.

Pierre, P. & Robert, S.F. (2004). *The Regulation of Emotion.* Routledge.

Plambeck, N. & Weber, K. (2009). CEO ambivalence and responses to strategic issues. *Organization Science,* 20, 993–1010.

Plambeck, N. & Weber, K. (2010). When the glass is half full and half empty: CEOs' ambivalent interpretations of strategic issues. *Strategic Management Journal,* 31, 689–710.

Polletta, F. & Jasper, J. M. (2001). Collective identity and social movements. *Annual Review of Sociology,* 27(1), 283–305.

Porac, J. F., Thomas, H., Wilson, F., Paton, D. & Kanfer, A. (1995). Rivalry and the industry model of Scottish knitwear producers. *Administrative Science Quarterly,* 40(2), 203–27.

Pouthier, V. (2017). Griping and joking as identification rituals and tools for engagement in cross-boundary team meetings. *Organization Studies,* 38(6), 753–74.

Pratt, M. G. (1998). To be or not to be? Central questions in organizational identification. In D. A. Whetten & P. C. Godfrey, eds., *Identity in Organizations: Building Theory Through Conversations.* Thousand Oaks, CA: Sage Publications.

Pratt, M. G. (2000). The good, the bad, and the ambivalent: Managing identification among Amway distributors. *Administrative Science Quarterly,* 45, 456–93.

Pratt, M. G. & Corley, K. G. (2007). Managing multiple organizational identities: On identity ambiguity, identity conflict, and members' reactions. In: C. Bartel, S. L. Blader & A. Wrzesniewski, eds., *Identity and the Modern Organization.* Mahwah, NJ: Lawrence Erlbaum Associates, 99–118.

Pratt, M. G., Rockmann, K. W. & Kaufmann, J. B. (2006) Constructing professional identity: The role of work and identity learning cycles in the customization of identity among medical residents. *Academy of Management Journal,* 49, 235–62.

Qureshi, I., Kistruck, G. M. & Bhatt, B. (2016). The enabling and constraining effects of social ties in the process of institutional entrepreneurship. *Organization Studies,* 37(3), 425–47.

Rafaeli, A. & Sutton, R. I. (1987). Expression of emotion as part of the work role. *Academy of Management Review,* 12, 23–37.

Rafaeli. A. & Sutton, R. I. (1989). The expression of emotion in organizational life. In L. L. Cummings & B. M. Staw, eds., *Research in Organizational Behavior,* Vol. U. Greenwich, CT: JAI Press, 1–42.

Rao, H., Monin, P. & Durand, R. (2003). Institutional change in Tocqueville: Nouvelle cuisine as an identity movement in French gastronomy. *American Journal of Sociology*, 108, 795–843.

Reckwitz, A. (2002). Toward a theory of social practices: A development in cultural theorizing. *European Journal of Social Theory*, 5, 234–63.

Reger, J. (2004). Organizational "emotion work" through consciousness-raising: An analysis of a feminist organization. *Qualitative Sociology*, 27, 205–22.

Rennstam, J. & Ashcraft, K. L. (2014). Knowing work: Cultivating a practice-based epistemology of knowledge in organization studies. *Human Relations*, 67, 3–25.

Rhee, E. Y. & Fiss, P. C. (2014). Framing controversial actions: Regulatory focus, source credibility, and stock market reaction to poison pill adoption. *Academy of Management Journal*, 57(6), 1734–58.

Rindova, V. P., Pollock, T. G. & Hayward, M. L. A. (2006). Celebrity firms: The social construction of market popularity. *Academy of Management Review*, 31, 50–71.

Riordan, M. H. & Williamson, O. E. (1985) Asset specificity and economic organization. *International Journal of Industrial Organization*, 3(4), 365–78.

Rivera, K. D. (2015). Emotional taint: Making sense of emotional dirty work at the U.S. Border Patrol. *Management Communication Quarterly*, 29, 198–228.

Roberts, A. & Zietsma, C. (2018). Working for an app: Organizational boundaries, roles and meaning of work in the "on-demand" economy. *Research in the Sociology of Organization* (57). Bingley, UK: Emerald Publishing, 195–225.

Rock, D. & Tang, Y. (2009). Neuroscience of engagement. *NeuroLeadership Journal*, 2, 1–8.

Rodrigues, S. B. & Collinson, D. L. (1995). "Having fun"? Humour as resistance in Brazil. *Organization Studies*, 16(5), 739–68.

Rouleau, L. (2005). Micro-practices of strategic sensemaking and sensegiving: How middle managers interpret and sell change every day. *Journal of Management Studies*, 42, 1413–41.

Rudat, A. & Budar, J. (2015). Making retweeting social: The influence of content and context information on sharing news in Twitter. *Computers in Human Behavior*, 46, 75–84.

Ruebottom, T. & Auster, E. R. (2018). Reflexive disembedding: Personal narratives, empowerment and the emotional dynamics of interstitial events. *Organization Studies*, 39(4), 467–90.

Rynes, S. L., Bartunek, J. M., Dutton, J. E. & Margolis, J. D. (2012). Care and compassion through an organizational lens: Opening up new possibilities. *Academy of Management Review*.

Salancik, G. R. (1995). WANTED: A good network theory of organization. *Administrative Science Quarterly*, 40(2), 345–49.

Samra-Fredericks, D. (2003). Strategizing as lived experience and strategists' everyday efforts to shape strategic direction. *Journal of Management Studies*, 40, 141–74.

Samra-Fredericks, D. (2004). Managerial elites making rhetorical and linguistic "moves" for a moving (emotional) display. *Human Relations*, 57, 1103–43.

Sandberg, J. & Tsoukas, H. (2015). Making sense of the sensemaking perspective: Its constituents, limitations, and opportunities for further development. *Journal of Organizational Behavior*, 36, S6–S32.

Schultz, M. & Hernes, T. (2013). A temporal perspective on organizational identity. *Organization Science*, 24, 1–21.

Schabram, K. & Maitlis, S. (2017). Negotiating the challenges of a calling: Emotion and enacted sensemaking in animal shelter work. *Academy of Management Journal*, 60, 584–609.

Schatzki, T. R., Knorr-Cetina, K. & Savigny, E. (2001). *The Practice Turn in Contemporary Theory*. London: Routledge, IX, 239.

Scheff, T. J. (2007). Politics of hidden emotions: Responses to a war memorial. *Peace and Conflict: Journal of Peace Psychology*, 13, 237–46.

Scheer, M. (2012), Are emotions a kind of practice (and is that what makes them have a history)? A Bourdieuian approach to understanding emotion. *History and Theory*, 51, 193–220.

Schein, E. (2004). *Organizational Culture and Leadership*. 3rd edn. San Francisco, CA: Jossey-Bass.

Schilke, O. & Cook, K. S. (2013). A cross-level process theory of trust development in interorganizational relationships. *Strategic Organization*, 11(3), 281–303.

Schrock, D., Holden, D. & Reid, L. (2004). Creating emotional resonance: Interpersonal emotion work and motivational framing in a transgender community. *Social Problems*, 51, 61–81.

Schüssler, E., Rüling, C. C. & Wittneben, B. B. F. (2014). On melting summits: The limitations of field-configuring events as catalysts of change in transnational climate policy. *Academy of Management Journal*, 57, 140–71.

Scott, W. R. (2001). *Institutions and Organizations*. Thousand Oaks, CA: Sage Publications.

Scott, W. R. (2014). *Institutions and Organizations: Ideas, Interests, and Identities*. Los Angeles: Sage Publications.

Selznick, P. (1957). *Leadership in Administration*. Berkeley, CA: University of California Press.

Seo, M. G. & Creed, W. E. D. (2002). Institutional contradictions, praxis, and institutional change: A dialectical perspective. *Academy of Management Review*, 27, 222–47.

Shane, S. & Cable, D. (2002). Network ties, reputation and the financing of new ventures. *Management Science*, 48, 364–81.

Shane, S. & Venkataraman, S. (2000). The promise of entrepreneurship as a field of research. *Academy of Management Review*, 25(1), 217–26.

Shepherd, D. A. (2009). Grief recovery from the loss of a family business: A multi-and meso-level theory. *Journal of Business Venturing*, 24(1), 81–97.

Shepherd, D. A. (2015). Party on! A call for entrepreneurship research that is more interactive, activity based, cognitively hot, compassionate, and prosocial. *Journal of Business Venturing*, 30(4), 489–507.

Shepherd, D. A., Patzelt, H. & Wolfe, M. (2011). Moving forward from project failure: Negative emotions, affective commitment and learning from the experience. *Academy of Management Journal*, 54(6), 1229–59.

Shipilov, A., Gulati, R., Kilduff, M., Li, S. & Tsai, W. (2014). Relational pluralism within and between organizations. *Academy of Management Journal*, 57(2), 449–59.

Sillince, J. & Shipton, H. (2013). More than a cognitive experience: Unfamiliarity, invalidation and emotion in organizational learning. *Journal of Management Inquiry*, 22(3), 342–55.

Simpson, B. & Marshall, N. (2010). The mutuality of emotions and learning in organizations. *Journal of Management Inquiry*, 19(4), 351–65.

Sine, W. & Lee, B. (2009). Tilting at windmills? The environmental movement and the emergence of the U.S. wind energy sector. *Administrative Science Quarterly* 54(1), 123–55.

Slade Shantz, A., Kistruck, G. & Zietsma, C. (2018). The opportunity not taken: The occupational identity of entrepreneurs in contexts of poverty. *Journal of Business Venturing*, 33(4), 416–37.

Sluss, D. M., van Dick, R. & Thompson, B. S. (2011). Role theory in organizations: A relational perspective. In *APA Handbook of Industrial and Organizational Psychology, Vol 1: Building and Developing the Organization*. Washington, DC: American Psychological Association, 505–34.

Smets, M., Aristidou, A. & Whittington, R. (2017). Toward a practice-driven institutionalism. In R. Greenwood, C. Oliver, T. B. Lawrence, et al., eds., *The Sage Handbook of Organizational Institutionalism*. 2nd edn. London: Sage Publications, 365–91.

Smircich, L. & Stubbart, C. (1985). Strategic management in an enacted world. *Academy of Management Review*, 10, 724–36.

Smollan, R. K. & Sayers, J. G. (2009). Organizational culture, change and emotions: A qualitative study. *Journal of Change Management*, 9(4), 435–57.

Snow, D. A., Burke, E., Rochford, J., et al. (1986). Frame alignment processes, micromobilizations, and movement participation. *American Sociological Review*, 51, 464–81.

Staggenborg, S. (2013). Institutionalization of social movements. In D. A. Snow, D. della Porta, B. Klandermans & D. McAdam, eds., *The Wiley-Blackwell Encyclopedia of Social and Political Movements*, Hoboken, NJ: Wiley-Blackwell.

Stam, W., Arzlanian, S. & Elfring, T. (2014). Social capital of entrepreneurs and small firm performance: A meta-analysis of contextual and methodological moderators. *Journal of Business Venturing*, 29(1), 152–73.

Stanley, D., Meyer, J. & Topolnytsky, L. (2005). Employee cynicism and resistance to organizational change. *Journal of Business and Psychology*, 19(4), 429–59.

Stein, A. (2001). Revenge of the shamed: Christian right's emotional culture war. In J. Goodwin, J. M. Jasper & F. Polletta, eds., *Passionate Politics: Emotions and Social Movements*. Chicago, IL: University of Chicago Press, 115–31.

Stets, J. E. & Trettevik, R. (2014). Emotions in identity theory. In J. E. Stets and J. H. Turner, eds., *Handbook of the Sociology of Emotions*. Vol. II. Dordrecht: Springer.

Stets, J. E. & Turner, J. H. (2014). Introduction. In J. E. Stets and J. H. Turner, eds., *Handbook of the Sociology of Emotions*. Vol. II. Dordrecht: Springer, pp. 1–7.

Stigliani, I. & Ravasi, D. (2012). Organizing thoughts and connecting brains: Material practices and the transition from individual to group-level prospective sensemaking. *Academy of Management Journal*, 55, 1232–59.

Suddaby, R. & Greenwood, R. (2005). Rhetorical strategies of legitimacy. *Administrative Science Quarterly*, 50, 35–67.

Suddaby, R., Hardy, C. & Huy, Q. N. (2011). Where are the new theories of organization? *Academy of Management Review*, 36, 236–46.

Summers-Effler, E. (2002). The Micro potential for social change: Emotion, consciousness, and social movement formation. *Sociological Theory*, 20, 41–60.

Summers-Effler, E. (2010). *Laughing Saints and Righteous Heroes: Emotional Rhythms in Social Movement Groups*. Chicago, IL: University of Chicago Press.

Sutton, R. & Rafaeli, A. (1988). Untangling the relationship between displayed emotions and organizational sales. *Academy of Management Journal*, 31, 461–87.

Swann, J. W. B., Johnson, R. E. & Bosson, J. K. (2009). Identity negotiation at work. *Research in Organizational Behavior*, 29, 81–109.

Swidler, A. (2001). *Talk of Love: How Culture Matters*. Chicago, IL:University of Chicago Press.

Tajfel, H. (1978). *Differentiation between Social Groups*. London: Academic Press.

Tajfel, H. (1982). *Social Identity and Inter-Group Relations*. Cambridge: Cambridge University Press.

Tasselli, S., Kilduff, M. & Menges, J. I. (2015). The microfoundations of organizational social networks: A review and an agenda for future research. *Journal of Management*, 41(5), 1361–87.

Taylor, V. (2013). Social movement participation in the global society: Identity, networks and emotions. In J. V. Stekelenburg, C. Roggeband & B. Klandermans, eds., *The Future of Social Movement Research*. Minneapolis, MN: University of Minnesota Press.

Taylor, V. & Rupp, L. (2002). Loving internationalism: The emotion culture of transnational women's organizations, 1888–1945. *Mobilization: An International Quarterly*, 7, 141–58.

Thompson, M. (2005). Structural and epistemic parameters in communities of practice. *Organization Science*, 16, 151–64.

Thompson, M. & Willmott, H. (2016). The social potency of affect: Identification and power in the immanent structuring of practice. *Human Relations*, 69, 483–506.

Thornborrow, T. & Brown, A. D. (2009). "Being regimented": Aspiration, discipline and identity work in the British parachute regiment. *Organization Studies*, 30, 355–76.

Thornton, P. H. & Ocasio, W. (1999). Institutional logics and the historical contingency of power in organizations: Executive succession in the higher education publishing industry, 1958–1990. *American Journal of Sociology*, 105, 801–43.

Thornton, P. H., Ocasio, W. & Lounsbury, M. (2012). *The Institutional Logics Perspective: A New Approach to Culture, Structure and Process*. Oxford: Oxford University Press.

Tobias, J. M., Mair, J. & Barbosa-Leiker, C. (2013). Toward a theory of transformative entrepreneuring: Poverty reduction and conflict resolution in Rwanda's entrepreneurial coffee sector. *Journal of Business Venturing*, 28, 728–42.

Toegel, G., Kilduff, M. & Anand, N. (2013). Emotion helping by managers: An emergent understanding of discrepant role expectations and outcomes. *Academy of Management Journal*, 56(2), 334–57.

Toubiana, M. (2014). Once in orange always in orange? The cognitive, emotional and material elements of de-identification and logic resilience. *Organization Studies*. Schulich School of Business: York University, 1–170.

Toubiana, M., Greenwood, R. & Zietsma, C. (2017). Beyond ethos: Outlining an alternate trajectory for emotional competence and investment. *Academy of Management Review*, 42, 551–56.

Toubiana, M. & Zietsma, C. (2017). The message is on the wall? Emotions, social media and the dynamics of institutional complexity. *Academy of Management Journal*, 60, 922–53.

Tracey, P. (2016). Spreading the word: The microfoundations of institutional persuasion and conversion. *Organization Science*, 27(4), 989–1009.

Tsai, W. (2002). Social structure of "coopetition" within a multiunit organization: Coordination, competition, and intraorganizational knowledge sharing. *Organization Science*, 13(2), 179–90.

Tsai, W. & Ghoshal, S. (1998). Social capital and value creation: The role of intrafirm networks. *Academy of Management Journal*, 41(4), 464–76.

Turchick-Hakak, L. (2014). Professionals in disguise: Identity work in situations of downward occupational transition. *Academy of Management Proceedings*, 1, 1641–46.

Turner, J. H. & Stets J. E. (2005). *The Sociology of Emotions*. Cambridge: Cambridge University Press.

Uy, M. A., Lin, K. J. & Ilies, R. (2017). Is it better to give or receive? The role of help in buffering the depleting effects of surface acting. *Academy of Management Journal*, 60(4), 1442–61.

Uzzi, B. (1997). Social structure and competition in interfirm networks: The paradox of embeddedness. *Administrative Science Quarterly*, 35–67.

Vaccaro, A. & Palazzo, G. (2015). Values against violence: Institutional change in societies dominated by organized crime. *Academy of Management Journal*, 58(4), 1075–1101.

Vaisey, S. & Lizardo, O. (2010). Can cultural worldviews influence network composition? *Social Forces*, 88(4), 1595–1618.

Vallas, S. P. & Cummins, E. R. (2015). Personal branding and identity norms in the popular business press: Enterprise culture in an age of precarity. *Organization Studies*, 36(3), 293–319.

Van Maanen, J. (1991). The smile factory: Work at Disneyland. In P. J. Frost, L. F. Moore, M. R. Louis, C. C. Lundberg & J. Martin, eds., *Reframing Organizational Culture*. Newbury Park, CA: Sage Publications.

Van Maanen, J. & Kunda, G. (1989). Real feelings – emotional expression and organizational culture. *Research in Organizational Behavior*, 11, 43–103.

Van Wierengen, M., Groenewegen, P. & Broese van Groenou, M. (2017). "We're all Florence Nightingales": Managers and nurses colluding in decoupling through contingent roles. *Journal of Professions and Organization*, 4, 241–60.

Van Wijk, J., Zietsma, C., Dorado, S., de Bakker, F. G. A. & Martí, I. (forthcoming). Social innovation: Integrating micro, meso and macro level insights from institutional theory. *Business & Society*.

Vergne, J. P. & Wry, T. (2014). Categorizing categorization research: Review, integration, and future directions. *Journal of Management Studies*, 51(1), 56–94.

Vickers, M. H. (2015). Stories, disability, and "dirty" workers: Creative writing to go beyond too few words. *Journal of Management Inquiry*, 24, 82–89.

Vince, R. (2001). Power and emotion in organizational learning. *Human Relations*, 54(10), 1325–51.

Vince, R. (2002). The impact of emotion on organizational learning. *Human Resource Development International*, 5(1), 73–85.

Vince, R. (2006). Being taken over: Managers' emotions and rationalizations during a company takeover. *Journal of Management Studies*, 43, 343–65.

Vince, R. (2010). Anxiety, politics and critical management education. *British Journal of Management*, 21(s1), s26–s39.

Vince, R. (in press). Illogics: The unconscious and institutional analysis. *Organization Studies*.

Vince, R. & Saleem, T. (2004). The impact of caution and blame on organizational learning. *Management Learning*, 35, 131–52.

Vogus, T. J., Rothman, N. B., Sutcliffe, K. M. & Weick, K. E. (2014). The affective foundations of high-reliability organizing. *Journal of Organizational Behavior*, 35(4), 592–96.

Voronov, M. (2014). Toward a toolkit for emotionalizing institutional theory. In *Emotions and the Organizational Fabric*. Bingley, UK: Emerald Publishing, 167–96.

Voronov, M. & Vince, R. (2012). Integrating emotions into the analysis of institutional work. *Academy of Management Review*, 37, 58–81.

Voronov, M. & Weber, K. (2016). The heart of institutions: Emotional competence and institutional actorhood. *Academy of Management Review*, 41, 456–78.

Voronov, M. & Weber, K. (2017). Emotional competence, institutional ethos and the heart of institutions. *Academy of Management Review*, 42, 556–60.

Voronov, M. & Yorks, L. (2015). "Did you notice that?" Theorizing differences in the capacity to apprehend institutional contradictions. *Academy of Management Review*, 40, 563–86.

Vough, H. (2012). Not all identifications are created equal: Exploring employee accounts for workgroup, organizational, and professional identification. *Organization Science*, 23, 778–800.

Wang, D., Sutcliffe, A. & Zeng, X. J. (2011). A trust-based multi-ego social network model to investigate emotion diffusion. *Social Network Analysis & Mining*, 1, 287 99.

Weber, M. (1978). *Economy and Society*, 212–54, 956–75.

Weber, K. & Glynn, M. A. (2006). Making sense with institutions: Context, thought and action in Karl Weick's theory. *Organization Studies* 27: 1639–60.

Weber, K., Heinze, K. & DeSoucey, M. (2008). Forage for thought: Mobilizing codes in the movement for grass-fed meat and dairy products. *Administrative Science Quarterly*, 53, 529–67.

Weick, K. E. (1979). *The Social Psychology of Organizing*. New York, NY: Random House.

Weick, K. E. (1993). The collapse of sensemaking in organizations: The Mann Gulch disaster. *Administrative Science Quarterly*, 38, 628–52.

Weick, K. E. (1995). *Sensemaking in Organizations*, Thousand Oaks, CA: Sage Publications.

Weik, E. (forthcoming). Value, affect and beauty: The Weird Sisters of institutionalist theory. A ritualist perspective. *European Management Journal*.

Welpe, I. M., Spörrle, M., Grichnik, D., Michl, T. & Audretsch, D. B. (2012). Emotions and opportunities: The interplay of opportunity evaluation, fear, joy, and anger as antecedent of entrepreneurial exploitation. *Entrepreneurship Theory and Practice*, 36(1), 69–96.

Wenger, E. (1998). *Communities of Practice: Learning, Meaning, and Identity*. Cambridge and New York, NY: Cambridge University Press.

Wharton, A. S. (2009). The sociology of emotional labor. *Annual Review of Sociology*, 35(1), 147–165.

Whittington, R. (2006). Completing the practice turn in strategy research. *Organization Studies*, 27, 613–34.

Wijaya, H. R. & Heugens, P. (2018). Give me a hallelujah! Amen! Institutional reproduction in the presence of moral perturbation and the dynamics of emotional investment. *Organization Studies*, 39(4), 491–514.

Williams, M. (2007). Building genuine trust through interpersonal emotion management: A threat regulation model of trust and collaboration across boundaries. *Academy of Management Review*, 32(2), 595–621.

Williamson, O. E. (1975). *Markets and Hierarchies: Analysis and Antitrust Implications*. New York, NY: Free Press.

Williamson, O. E. (1993). Calculativeness, trust, and economic organization. *Journal of Law and Economics*, 36 (1, Part 2), 453–86.

Wright, A. L., Zammuto, R. F. & Liesch, P. W. (2017). Maintaining the values of a profession: Institutional work and moral emotions in the emergency department. *Academy of Management Journal*, 60, 200–37.

Wry, T., Cobb, J. A. & Aldrich, H. E. (2013). More than a metaphor: Assessing the historical legacy of resource dependence and its contemporary promise as a theory of environmental complexity. *Academy of Management Annals*, 7(1), 441–48.

Wry, T., Lounsbury, M. & Glynn, M. A. (2011). Legitimating nascent collective identities: Coordinating cultural entrepreneurship. *Organization Science*, 22(2), 449–63.

Wry, T., Lounsbury, M., & Jennings, P. D. (2014). Hybrid vigor: Securing venture capital by spanning categories in nanotechnology. *Academy of Management Journal*, 57(5), 1309–33.

Young, M.P. (2001). A revolution of the soul: Transformative experiences and immediate abolition. In J. Goodwin, J. M. Jasper & F. Polletta, eds., *Passionate Politics: Emotions and Social Movements*. Chicago, IL: University of Chicago Press, 99–114.

Zaheer, A., McEvily, B. & Perrone, V. (1998). Does trust matter? Exploring the effects of interorganizational and interpersonal trust on performance. *Organization Science*, 9(2), 141–59.

Zajonc, R. B. (1980). Feeling and thinking: Preferences need no inferences. *American Psychologist*, 35(2), 151–75.

Zelizer, V. A. (2007). Pasts and futures of economic sociology. *American Behavioral Scientist*, 50, 1056–69.

Zhixing, X. & Tsui, A. S. (2007). When brokers may not work: The cultural contingency of social capital in Chinese high-tech firms. *Administrative Science Quarterly*, 52(1), 1–31.

Zietsma, C. & Lawrence, T. B. (2010). Institutional work in the transformation of an organizational field: The interplay of boundary work and practice work. *Administrative Science Quarterly*, 55, 189–221.

Zietsma, C. & Toubiana, M. (2018). The valuable, the constitutive, and the energetic: Exploring the impact and importance of studying emotions and institutions. *Organization Studies*, 39(4), 427–43.

Zietsma, C. & Toubiana, M. (forthcoming). Emotions as the glue, the fuel and the rust of social innovation. In G. George, T. Baker, H. Joshi & P. Tracey, eds., *Handbook of Social Innovation*. Cheltenham, UK: Edward Elgar Publishing.

Zilber, T. B. (2002). Institutionalization as an interplay between actions, meanings, and actors: The case of a rape crisis center in Israel. *Academy of Management Journal*, 45, 234–54.

Zilber, T. B. (2017). A call for "strong" multimodal research in institutional theory. *Research in the Sociology of Organizations*, 54, 63–84.

# Acknowledgments

We'd like to thank some subject matter experts that reviewed our work and gave us advice on particular sections. These included Melissa Cardon, Shon Hiatt, Mike Lounsbury, Sally Maitlis, Gianpiero Petriglieri, Christopher Steele and two anonymous reviewers. In addition, we'd like to thank Sandra Reimer, Haley Parkhill, Bob Reimer, Hazel Reimer and Rebecca Korsten for editorial and formatting assistance. Finally, we'd like to thank Royston Greenwood for some excellent feedback, and both Royston and Nelson Phillips for their patience in waiting for an Element that was a little harder than we thought to produce.

# About the Authors

**Charlene Zietsma** is Associate Professor, Management and Organization at the Smeal College of Business, Pennsylvania State University. She studies emotions and institutions, institutional change processes, field theory and entrepreneurship. Her work has been published in *Administrative Science Quarterly, Academy of Management Journal, Academy of Management Review, Organization Science, Organization Studies, Journal of Business Venturing* and others. In 2016, she was awarded the ASQ Scholarly Contribution Award for significant impact on the field of organization studies. She is a Senior Editor for *Organization Studies*, has been guest editor for *Business & Society, Research in the Sociology of Organizations, Strategic Organization* and *Organization Studies,* and serves on the editorial board for several other journals.

**Madeline Toubiana** is an Assistant Professor of Strategic Management and Organization at the University of Alberta, School of Business and is the current Southam Faculty Fellow. Her research focuses on the role emotions, complexity and stigmatization play in processes of social change. To understand the dynamics of social change, she examines the intersection and interaction between social actors and institutional systems. Some of her previous and current work examines this topic in the context of social entrepreneurship, academia, social media, the Canadian prison system and the sex trade. Her research has been published in the *Academy of Management*

*Journal, Academy Management Review, Organization Studies, Journal of Management History,* and *Management Learning,* among others. She has also guest edited a special themed section in *Organization Studies* on the topic of emotions and institutions.

**Maxim Voronov** is Professor of Organization Studies at the Schulich School of Business, York University. He is interested in institutional stability and change, emotions and the construction and use of cultural resources. Maxim's work appears in such leading management journals as *Academy of Management Review, Academy of Management Journal, Journal of Management Studies, Human Relations,* and *Organization,* among others. He is on the editorial boards of *Academy of Management Review, Academy of Management Journal,* and *Journal of Management Studies.*

**Anna Roberts** is a doctoral candidate in the Management and Organization Department at the Smeal College of Business, Pennsylvania State University, United States. Anna studies inequality, the future of work, new organizational forms, and the microfoundations of institutions, including emotions. She earned her B.A. from Rice University, graduating magna cum laude and was the sole recipient of the Muhammad Yunus Commencement Award for Humanitarian Leadership. Prior to joining academia, she led the West Coast Regulatory Practice Area at Gerson Lehrman Group.

Cambridge Elements $\equiv$

# Organization Theory

## Elements in the Series

Printed in the United States
By Bookmasters